FEEDBACK TO FEEDFORWARD

A GUIDE TO PROVIDING EFFECTIVE FEEDBACK TO STUDENTS

DR MEENAKSHI NARULA

Made with ♥ on the Notion Press Platform
www.notionpress.com

To all those who strive for growth and development, Who believe in the power of feedback, And who embrace the future with an open mind and a willingness to learn.

This book is dedicated to you.

May the insights and strategies within these pages help you to transform feedback into feedforward, to turn criticism into opportunity, and to move ever closer towards your goals.

And to Dr. Meenakshi Narula, whose passion and expertise have made this book possible, thank you for your tireless dedication to helping others grow and thrive. Your insights and guidance will undoubtedly have a profound impact on countless individuals and organizations, both now and for years to come.

Contents

Foreword *ix*

Preface *xi*

Acknowledgements *xiii*

Prologue *xv*

About The Author *xvii*

1. What's Feedback To Feedforward? 1
2. Some Tips For Using Ready-to-use Feedback Comments 2
3. Behaviour Feedback Comments For Students 3
4. Classroom Management Comments For Students 4
5. Notebook Comments For Students 5
6. Map Work Feedback Comments 6
7. Year-end Citation Comments For Students 7
8. Leadership Feedback Comments For Students 8
9. Comments Regarding Immaculate Uniform 10
10. Feedback For Singing Club Students-performing Arts 11
11. Feedback For Dance Club Students- Performing Arts 12
12. Feedback For Culinary Club Students 14
13. Feedback For Oratory Skills 15
14. Feedback For Writing Skills 17
15. Feedback For Classroom Revision 18
16. Feedback For Class Test Performance 19
17. Feedback For Science Test 20
18. Feedback For Math Test 21
19. Feedback For Grammar And Vocabulary 22
20. Feedback For Spoken English 23
21. Feedback For Communication Skills 24
22. Feedback For Games And Sports 25
23. Feedback For Reading Skills (dear Club) 26
24. Feedback For Comprehension Skills 27
25. Feedback For Writing Skills 28
26. Feedback For Teamwork And Collaboration 30
27. Feedback For Listening Skills 31
28. Feedback For Show And Tell 32
29. Feedback For Psychomotor Skills 33
30. Feedback For Affective Domain 34
31. Feedback For Cognitive Skills 35

Contents

32. Feedback For Life Skills 36
33. Comprehensive Feedback For Adolescents 38
34. Comprehensive Feedback For Kindergarteners 39
35. Feedback For Formative Assessments 40
36. Feedback For Routine Assessments 41
37. Feedback For Physics Students 43
38. Feedback For Chemistry Students 44
39. Feedback For Biology Students 45
40. Feedback For Science Diagrams 46
41. Feedback For Powerpoint Presentations 47
42. Feedback For Kindergarten Students On Graduation Day 48
43. Feedback For Subject Concept Clarity 49
44. Feedback For Technological Skills 50
45. Feedback For Debate 51
46. Feedback For Group Discussions 52
47. Feedback For Kindergarten Report Cards 53
48. Feedback For Primary School Report Cards 54
49. Feedback For Middle School Report Cards 55
50. Feedback For High School Report Cards 56
51. Feedback For Kindergarten Notebook Correction 57
52. Feedback For Primary School Notebooks 58
53. Feedback For Middle School Notebooks 59
54. Feedback For High School Notebooks 60
55. Comprehensive Feedback For Languages (english/ Hindi/ Punjabi...any Languages) 61
56. Comprehensive Feedback For Mathematics 62
57. Comprehensive Feedback For Science 63
58. Comprehensive Feedback For Social Science 64
59. Feedback For Kindergarten Activities 65
60. Feedback For Primary School Activities 66
61. Feedback For Senior Students 67
62. Feedback For Art-integrated Learning 69
63. Feedback For Co-curricular Activities 70
64. Encouraging Feedback For Students 71
65. Notebook Remarks For Homework By Teachers 72
66. Revision Work Feedback Comments 73
67. Literature Work Feedback For Students 74

Contents

68. Grammar And Vocabulary Usage Feedback For Students 75
69. Feedback For Geometry Skills 76
70. Feedback For Algebra 77
71. Feedback For Science Project 78
72. Feedback For Art Work 79
73. Feedback For Various Mi Skills (multiple Intelligences) 80
74. Feedback Comments On Rhyme Recitation 81
75. Feedback For Storytelling 82
76. Feedback On Poster Making 83
77. Feedback On Slogan Writing 84
78. Feedback On Roleplay 85
79. Feedback On Clay Moulding 86
80. Feedback For Effective Library Usage 87
81. Feedback For Creativity And Innovation 88
82. Feedback For Problem-solving Skills 89
End Note 91
Mentoring The Mentors 93
Our Motto- "to Accelerate Your Learning Curve" 95

Foreword

As someone who has spent many years in leadership roles, I can attest to the transformative power of feedback. When delivered thoughtfully and constructively, feedback has the ability to unlock potential, drive growth, and inspire change.

But too often, feedback is viewed as negative, something to be dreaded or avoided altogether. That's where Dr. Meenakshi Narula's new book, "Feedback to Feedforward," comes in. In this insightful and practical guide, Dr. Narula provides a roadmap for transforming feedback into an opportunity for growth and development.

Drawing on her extensive experience as a consultant and coach, Dr. Narula provides practical strategies for receiving and giving feedback, as well as techniques for turning feedback into a powerful tool for forward momentum. From reframing our mindset around feedback to utilizing feedback to set goals and drive progress, this book is a must-read for anyone looking to unlock their full potential.

But perhaps what I find most compelling about "Feedback to Feedforward" is Dr. Narula's emphasis on the importance of creating a culture of feedback. By fostering a culture where feedback is valued and encouraged, organizations and individuals alike can tap into the power of feedback to drive continuous improvement and innovation.

In short, "Feedback to Feedforward" is a valuable resource for anyone looking to unlock their full potential and create a culture of growth and development. I highly recommend this book to anyone who is committed to their own growth, as well as the growth of those around them.

Dr Sanjiv Narula

Preface

Providing effective feedback is an essential part of the learning process for students. As educators, we have a responsibility to guide and support our students as they navigate their academic journey, and feedback plays a crucial role in this process. The feedback we give helps our students identify their strengths, areas for improvement, and encourages them to take ownership of their learning.

This book is designed to assist educators in providing meaningful feedback to their students. The feedback comments provided in this book are intended to be used as a starting point for teachers to develop their own feedback comments that are specific and relevant to their students' needs. It is important to note that these comments are not a "one size fits all" solution, as every student has unique strengths and weaknesses, and feedback should be tailored to meet their individual needs.

The comments in this book are organized by age group, from kindergarten to high school, and cover a range of subjects and skills, including writing, math, science, and social skills. These comments can be used for report cards, progress reports, or daily classroom feedback.

The goal of this book is to provide educators with a valuable resource that will help them provide meaningful feedback to their students. Effective feedback can help students grow and thrive academically and personally, and we hope that this book will be a useful tool in achieving this goal.

Acknowledgements

I would like to express my gratitude to all the educators who directly or indirectly contributed to this book on feedback to feedforward comments for all grades. Without their valuable input and expertise, this book would not have been possible.

I would also like to thank the students who have been the inspiration for this book. Your dedication to learning and growth has motivated us to develop this resource to support your academic journey.

Special thanks to my colleagues at my organisation who have provided us with support and encouragement throughout the process of writing this book. Your feedback and suggestions have been invaluable.

Lastly, I would like to thank my family and a special friend for the love and support during the writing process. Without their unwavering support, this book would not have been possible.

Thank you to everyone who has contributed to this book, and we hope that it will be a useful resource for educators and students alike as they work to achieve their academic goals and reach their full potential.

Dr Meenakshi Narula

Principal

Prologue

Feedback is a powerful tool that can either inspire or discourage growth and development. As a consultant and coach, I have seen firsthand the impact that feedback can have on individuals and organizations. Too often, however, feedback is viewed as negative, something to be avoided or dreaded.

That's why I wrote this book - "Feedback to Feedforward" - to help individuals and organizations transform feedback into an opportunity for growth and development. Drawing on my years of experience as a consultant and coach, as well as the latest research in the field of psychology and organizational behavior, I provide practical strategies for receiving and giving feedback, as well as techniques for turning feedback into a powerful tool for forward momentum.

In this book, I explore how our mindset around feedback can either limit or enhance our potential for growth, and provide practical tools for shifting our mindset towards a more constructive and growth-oriented perspective. I also delve into the mechanics of feedback, exploring how to give and receive feedback effectively, and providing strategies for turning feedback into an opportunity for goal-setting and progress.

But perhaps most importantly, I emphasize the importance of creating a culture of feedback. By fostering a culture where feedback is valued and encouraged, organizations and individuals alike can tap into the power of feedback to drive continuous improvement and innovation.

At its core, "Feedback to Feedforward" is about embracing the power of feedback as a tool for growth and development. It's about taking a proactive approach to feedback, and turning it into an opportunity for progress and success. I invite you to join me on this journey, and to discover the transformative power of feedback for yourself.

About The Author

Dr. Meenakshi Narula (Principal, Shemford Futuristic K12 School), 2020-till date) is an experienced educator, author, and Youtuber with a passion for helping students and teachers achieve their academic potential. With a doctorate in Education, Dr. Narula has spent many years working in the field of education, both as a teacher and as an administrator.

Throughout her career, Dr. Narula has focused on developing innovative and effective teaching strategies that help students learn and grow. She has a particular interest in the role that feedback can play in supporting student learning and achievement.

Dr. Narula has written various articles on feedback, classroom routines, and revision strategies, including the widely acclaimed "Feedback to Feedforward: A Guide to Providing Effective Feedback to Students." This book has become a valuable resource for educators of all levels, from kindergarten through high/secondary/sr. secondary school.

In addition to her work as an author, Dr. Narula is also a sought-after speaker and edu-consultant. She has provided training and professional development to educators across the globe, helping them to develop effective feedback strategies and support student learning.

Overall, Dr. Meenakshi Narula's expertise in the field of education and her passion for supporting student learning have made her a respected and influential figure in the world of education. Her work continues to inspire and guide educators as they work to help their students achieve academic success.

CHAPTER ONE

What's Feedback to Feedforward?

Feedback to feedforward is a concept that focuses on providing feedback that helps individuals improve their future performance. It is a way to move away from focusing solely on past performance and instead use feedback as a tool for growth and development. Here are some tips for providing feedback to feedforward:

Focus on future goals: When providing feedback, focus on the individual's future goals and how they can improve their performance to achieve those goals.

Be specific: Provide specific feedback on areas where the individual can improve, and provide actionable suggestions on how they can improve.

Use positive language: Use positive language to encourage individuals to continue to work hard and improve. Avoid negative language or criticism that could discourage individuals.

Encourage self-reflection: Encourage individuals to reflect on their own performance and identify areas for improvement. This will help them take ownership of their learning and take steps to improve their performance.

Provide ongoing support: Offer ongoing support and guidance to individuals as they work to improve their performance. This can include coaching, mentoring, or additional training.

Create a safe and supportive environment: Create a safe and supportive environment where individuals feel comfortable seeking feedback and taking risks to improve their performance.

Celebrate progress: Celebrate progress and accomplishments along the way. This will help individuals stay motivated and continue to work hard to improve their performance.

By providing feedback to feedforward, individuals can use feedback as a tool for growth and development. This can help them achieve their future goals and reach their full potential.

CHAPTER TWO

Some tips for using ready-to-use feedback comments

Choose comments that are relevant to your students: Look for comments that are specific to the age group and subject area you teach. This will help ensure that the comments are relevant to your students' needs.

Personalize the comments: While ready-to-use comments are helpful, they should not be used verbatim. Take the time to personalize the comments to the specific student you are providing feedback to.

Be specific: Avoid vague or general comments that do not provide specific feedback on a student's performance. Instead, focus on specific strengths and areas for improvement.

Use positive language: When providing feedback, use positive language that will encourage students to continue to work hard and improve. Avoid negative language or criticism that could discourage students.

Balance strengths and areas for improvement: When providing feedback, it is important to balance comments that highlight a student's strengths with comments that address areas for improvement. This will help students understand where they excel and where they need to focus their efforts.

Provide actionable suggestions: Along with feedback on performance, provide actionable suggestions on how the student can improve. This will help them take ownership of their learning and take steps to improve their performance.

Use feedback as a teaching tool: Feedback is not just a tool for assessment, but also a teaching tool. Use feedback to help students understand how they can improve their performance and develop their skills.

Overall, ready-to-use feedback comments can be a helpful resource for educators. By personalizing the comments and using them as a starting point for personalized feedback, educators can provide students with meaningful feedback that helps them grow and thrive academically and personally.

CHAPTER THREE

Behaviour feedback comments for students

Here are some behaviour feedback comments that teachers could use to provide feedback to students:

- Great job! Your behaviour in class is consistently excellent.
- You consistently show respect and kindness to your classmates and teachers.
- Your positive attitude and enthusiasm for learning are contagious.
- You are a great role model for your peers in terms of your behaviour and work ethic.
- You consistently demonstrate responsibility and accountability for your actions.
- You are always willing to help others and contribute to the class.
- Your ability to follow directions and take feedback is impressive.
- You consistently demonstrate self-control and manage your emotions well.
- Your ability to work collaboratively with others is strong.
- Keep up the great work! Your positive behaviour is appreciated by everyone.
- Your willingness to try new things and take risks is impressive.
- Your ability to stay focused and on-task is admirable.
- Your behaviour consistently demonstrates integrity and honesty.
- You are always willing to take responsibility for your mistakes and make things right.
- Your behaviour reflects a deep sense of empathy and compassion towards others. Well done!

CHAPTER FOUR

Classroom Management comments for students

Here are some classroom management comments that teachers could use to provide feedback to students:

- Great job following our class rules and expectations.
- Your ability to stay on-task and focused during class is impressive.
- You consistently demonstrate respect towards your classmates and teachers.
- Your willingness to participate and contribute to class discussions is appreciated.
- Your use of classroom materials and resources is responsible and respectful.
- You consistently arrive on time and are prepared for class.
- Your ability to work independently and stay engaged in class is impressive.
- Your positive attitude towards learning and class activities is contagious.
- You are a great role model for your peers in terms of classroom behavior and management.
- Keep up the great work! Your positive behavior and cooperation make our classroom a better place.
- Your willingness to follow directions and take feedback is admirable.
- Your ability to manage your time and prioritize tasks is impressive.
- Your behavior consistently demonstrates responsibility and accountability.
- Your use of technology and digital resources in the classroom is respectful and appropriate.
- Your behavior reflects a deep sense of empathy and understanding towards others. Well done!

CHAPTER FIVE

Notebook comments for students

Here are some notebook comments that teachers could use to provide feedback to students:

- Great job keeping your notes organized and legible.
- Your notes are thorough and well-organized. It's clear that you've put a lot of effort into them.
- Your diagrams and sketches are neat and clearly labeled.
- Your use of color and highlighting helps to emphasize important points in your notes.
- Your notes show a strong understanding of the concepts covered in class.
- Your use of abbreviations and shorthand makes your notes easy to read and review.
- Your notes show strong attention to detail and a dedication to learning.
- Your notes show creativity and imagination in the way you present information.
- Your use of examples and real-world applications helps to deepen your understanding of the material.
- Keep up the great work! Your notes are well-organized and show a commitment to learning.
- Your notes reflect a deep understanding of the material and a willingness to engage with the content.
- Your notes show a strong ability to synthesize information and make connections between different topics.
- Your notes demonstrate a mastery of the vocabulary and terminology used in the subject.
- Your notes show an ability to identify and prioritize the most important information.
- Your notes reflect a strong work ethic and a dedication to academic success. Well done!

CHAPTER SIX

Map work Feedback Comments

Here are some map work feedback comments that teachers could use to provide feedback to students:

- Great job! Your map work is accurate and detailed.
- Your ability to read and interpret maps is impressive.
- Your maps are neatly drawn and clearly labeled.
- Your use of color and shading helps to differentiate between different features on the map.
- Your maps show a strong understanding of the geography and topography of the area.
- Your use of scale and key helps to provide context and clarity to your maps.
- Your ability to identify and mark important landmarks on the map is impressive.
- Your maps show a creative and imaginative approach to representing geographic information.
- Your ability to use digital tools and resources to create maps is impressive.
- Keep up the great work! Your map work is accurate and informative.
- Your maps reflect a deep understanding of the material and a willingness to engage with the content.
- Your maps demonstrate a mastery of the vocabulary and terminology used in the subject.
- Your maps show an ability to synthesize information and present it in a clear and concise manner.
- Your maps show an attention to detail and a dedication to getting things right.
- Your map work reflects a strong work ethic and a dedication to academic success. Well done!

CHAPTER SEVEN

Year-end Citation Comments for Students

Here are some year-end citation comments that teachers could use to acknowledge and recognize students' hard work throughout the school year:

- You consistently demonstrated a strong work ethic and dedication to your studies throughout the year. Well done!
- Your positive attitude towards learning and class activities is commendable.
- Your ability to think critically and creatively about the material we covered is impressive.
- You consistently went above and beyond in your academic pursuits and extracurricular activities.
- Your use of feedback and willingness to take constructive criticism has helped you to grow and improve throughout the year.
- Your leadership and collaboration skills have been an asset to our classroom and school community.
- Your passion for learning and growth is truly inspiring. Keep up the great work!
- Your commitment to academic success and personal growth has not gone unnoticed. Well done!
- Your kindness and respect towards your classmates and teachers is appreciated and admired.
- Your hard work and determination have paid off this year. Congratulations on a job well done!
- Your enthusiasm and curiosity for the material we covered is truly impressive.
- Your growth and progress throughout the year have been remarkable. Keep up the great work!
- Your perseverance and resilience in the face of challenges is admirable.
- Your dedication to academic excellence and personal growth is truly inspiring.
- Congratulations on a successful school year. Your hard work, dedication, and achievements have not gone unnoticed. Well done!

CHAPTER EIGHT

Leadership Feedback comments for Students

Here are some leadership feedback comments that teachers could use to provide feedback to students:

- Your leadership skills are truly impressive. You have the ability to motivate and inspire others to achieve their best.
- Your ability to communicate effectively and delegate tasks has been instrumental in the success of our group.
- You demonstrate a high level of emotional intelligence and empathy towards your peers, making you a natural leader.
- Your willingness to listen to feedback and take constructive criticism has helped you to improve as a leader throughout the year.
- You show a commitment to inclusivity and diversity in your leadership approach, making everyone feel valued and included.
- Your ability to remain calm and focused under pressure has been essential to the success of our team.
- You have a natural ability to identify the strengths of your teammates and utilize them to achieve our shared goals.
- Your willingness to take on challenges and try new things has been an inspiration to others in our group.
- You consistently lead by example, demonstrating a strong work ethic and commitment to excellence.
- Your positive attitude and enthusiasm for our projects and activities have been infectious and motivating to everyone around you.
- Your ability to collaborate and work as a team has been instrumental in the success of our group.
- Your leadership has helped to create a positive and supportive environment for everyone in our group.
- Your commitment to the values and goals of our group has been unwavering, making you a natural and effective leader.
- You consistently demonstrate a growth mindset, seeking out new challenges and opportunities to learn and improve as a leader.

- Your leadership skills have been instrumental in our success this year. Thank you for your dedication and hard work.

CHAPTER NINE

Comments regarding Immaculate Uniform

Here are some feedback comments that teachers could use to provide feedback to students regarding their immaculate uniform:

- Your uniform looks fantastic! Your attention to detail and dedication to presenting yourself well is commendable.
- Your immaculate uniform is a reflection of your respect for our school and the values it represents.
- Your uniform looks clean, crisp and tidy, making you a great representative of our school.
- Your effort to keep your uniform immaculate shows your pride and commitment to being a student at our school.
- Your attention to the uniform policy and ensuring that you are always properly dressed reflects your commitment to the school community.
- Your uniform looks sharp and well put together, showing that you are ready to take on the day ahead.
- Your commitment to presenting yourself well through your uniform demonstrates a high level of professionalism and maturity.
- Your immaculate uniform is a reflection of your commitment to personal responsibility and attention to detail.
- Your uniform looks great, and it is clear that you take pride in your appearance and in representing our school.
- Your attention to detail in keeping your uniform neat and tidy is impressive and is noticed and appreciated by your teachers and peers.
- Your uniform looks impeccable, reflecting your respect for the school and the community it represents.
- Your immaculate uniform is a testament to your discipline and dedication to being the best version of yourself.
- Your commitment to maintaining a clean and neat uniform sets a great example for your peers.
- Your uniform looks great, and your attention to detail and presentation is a credit to your personal values and the values of our school.
- Your immaculate uniform reflects your pride in our school and your commitment to being a responsible and respectful member of our community. Well done!

CHAPTER TEN

Feedback for Singing Club Students-Performing Arts

Here are some feedback comments that teachers could use to provide feedback to students regarding their singing:

- Your singing is beautiful! Your voice is clear and strong, and you have a natural talent for singing.
- Your singing has improved so much since the beginning of the year! You have worked hard to develop your vocal skills and it shows.
- Your tone and pitch are excellent, and you have a great sense of rhythm.
- Your ability to express emotions through your singing is outstanding. You have a natural ability to connect with your audience.
- Your attention to dynamics and phrasing in your singing is impressive. You have a great understanding of how to use your voice to create a powerful effect.
- Your ability to harmonize and blend with other singers is fantastic. You have a great ear for music.
- Your singing is confident and expressive. You have a stage presence that captures the attention of your audience.
- Your musicality and understanding of the song you are singing are evident in your performance. You have a real talent for interpreting music.
- Your singing is impressive, and your passion for music is inspiring to others.
- Your singing has improved greatly, and it is clear that you have been practicing and working hard to develop your skills.
- Your voice is unique and beautiful, and your singing has a distinctive style that sets you apart.
- Your ability to perform different styles of music is impressive. You are versatile and adapt well to different genres.
- Your vocal control and range are impressive. You have a natural ability to hit high notes with ease.
- Your singing is expressive and emotive, capturing the essence of the song you are performing.
- Your singing is excellent, and you have a real talent for music. Keep up the great work!

CHAPTER ELEVEN

Feedback for Dance Club Students-Performing Arts

Here are some feedback comments that teachers could use to provide feedback to students regarding their dancing:

- Your dance performance was outstanding! You have a great sense of rhythm and your movements were fluid and graceful.
- You have improved so much since the beginning of the year! Your dance technique has developed significantly and it shows in your performance.
- Your choreography and musicality are excellent. You have a natural ability to express yourself through movement.
- Your ability to work with others in a group dance is fantastic. You blend well with your peers and your teamwork is impressive.
- Your stage presence is captivating. You have a real talent for engaging with your audience and conveying emotion through your dance.
- Your attention to detail in your dance performance is impressive. You have a great understanding of the movements and the timing required to execute them properly.
- Your energy and enthusiasm on stage are infectious. You bring a great energy to your dance performance and inspire others to perform their best.
- Your passion for dance is evident in your performance. You have a real love for the art form and it shows in your dedication and commitment to your craft.
- Your dance skills are exceptional. You have a natural talent for movement and your dance technique is flawless.
- Your creativity in your dance performance is outstanding. You have a unique style and approach to dance that is truly inspiring.
- Your flexibility and agility in your dance movements are impressive. You have a great range of motion and can execute difficult movements with ease.
- Your ability to express emotion through your dance is powerful. You have a real talent for conveying the mood and feeling of the dance piece.

- Your dance performance was breathtaking. Your movements were precise and your performance was captivating.
- Your rhythm and timing are impeccable. You have a natural ability to stay on beat and your dance performance is always in sync with the music.
- Your dance performance was impressive, and you have a real talent for dance. Keep up the great work!

CHAPTER TWELVE

Feedback for Culinary Club Students

Here are some feedback comments for culinary club students:

- Your attention to detail is impressive. From the presentation of the dishes to the use of fresh ingredients, you are truly dedicated to creating high-quality dishes.

- You have a natural talent for cooking. Your ability to combine flavors and ingredients to create unique and delicious dishes is truly impressive.

- Your teamwork and collaboration skills are outstanding. You work well together and support one another in the kitchen, making the cooking process efficient and enjoyable.

- Your passion for cooking is evident in everything you do. You are always eager to try new recipes and techniques, and your enthusiasm is contagious.

- You are not afraid to take risks and experiment with new flavors and ingredients. This shows a willingness to learn and grow as a chef.

- You have a strong sense of creativity in the kitchen. Your ability to think outside the box and come up with unique dishes is impressive.

- Your positive attitude and willingness to learn are truly appreciated. You take feedback well and are always eager to improve your skills.

Overall, you are a talented and dedicated group of culinary club students. Keep up the great work and continue to challenge yourselves in the kitchen!

CHAPTER THIRTEEN

Feedback for Oratory Skills

Here are some feedback comments that teachers could use to provide feedback to students regarding their oratory skills:

- Your voice projection and clarity were excellent. You spoke with confidence and made sure everyone in the audience could hear and understand you.
- You had a great sense of pacing and emphasis in your speech. Your use of tone and inflection really brought your message to life.
- Your eye contact and body language were engaging. You maintained good eye contact with the audience and your gestures and posture were confident and natural.
- Your use of rhetorical devices and persuasive techniques was impressive. You effectively used rhetorical questions, repetition, and other techniques to persuade and captivate the audience.
- You demonstrated great knowledge of the subject matter and communicated it clearly and concisely. Your speech was informative and easy to follow.
- You had a clear structure and organization in your speech. Your introduction, main points, and conclusion were well thought out and effectively delivered.
- Your use of personal anecdotes and stories added depth and authenticity to your speech. Your audience could relate to your experiences and understand the message better.
- Your use of humour and wit made your speech entertaining and engaging. You had the audience laughing and kept their attention throughout.
- Your use of language and vocabulary was impressive. You demonstrated a wide range of vocabulary and used it in a way that was appropriate and effective.
- Your speech had a strong impact on the audience. You conveyed your message with passion and conviction and left a lasting impression on the audience.
- Your use of visual aids, such as slides or props, enhanced your speech and made it more engaging for the audience.
- You effectively responded to questions and comments from the audience. You demonstrated a deep understanding of the topic and provided thoughtful and well-reasoned responses.

- Your speech was well-researched and demonstrated a deep understanding of the topic. You used credible sources and evidence to support your arguments.
- Your speech was well rehearsed, and you demonstrated great delivery. You spoke with confidence and authority.
- Your oratory skills are impressive, and you have a real talent for public speaking. Keep up the great work and continue to hone your skills!

CHAPTER FOURTEEN

Feedback for Writing Skills

Here are some feedback comments that teachers could use to provide feedback to students regarding their letter-writing skills:

- Your letter was well-organized and followed the appropriate structure for a formal letter. Your introduction, body, and conclusion were clear and effective.
- You used appropriate tone and language for the intended audience and purpose of the letter. Your language was professional and respectful.
- You demonstrated a good understanding of the conventions of letter writing, including formatting, salutation, and closing.
- Your writing was clear and concise, and effectively communicated the message you intended to convey.
- You demonstrated good use of grammar, spelling, and punctuation. Your letter was free of errors that might detract from its overall effectiveness.
- You effectively used evidence and examples to support your arguments and make your case. Your writing was persuasive and well-supported.
- Your letter demonstrated a good level of research and preparation. You had a clear understanding of the topic and your arguments were well-informed.
- You demonstrated good attention to detail in your writing. Your letter was carefully crafted and edited for clarity and effectiveness.
- You showed creativity and originality in your letter writing. Your writing was engaging and stood out from others.
- Your letter was engaging and compelling. It was clear that you put thought and effort into crafting a letter that would be effective and impactful.
- You demonstrated good communication skills in your letter writing. You effectively conveyed your ideas and made your message clear and memorable.
- Your letter-writing skills have improved significantly over time. Keep up the good work and continue to practice and refine your skills.

CHAPTER FIFTEEN

Feedback for Classroom Revision

Here are some feedback comments that teachers could use to provide feedback to students regarding their classroom revision skills:

- Your revision techniques were effective in helping you to master the material. You showed good focus and commitment to your studies.

- You showed good organization and planning skills in your revision. You had a clear plan of action and followed it through effectively.

- You demonstrated good time management skills in your revision. You made the most of your study time and used it wisely.

- Your revision notes were clear, concise, and well-organized. You effectively summarized the key concepts and ideas you needed to understand.

- You demonstrated a good understanding of the material and were able to apply it effectively in your revision.

- You effectively used a variety of study resources, including textbooks, notes, online resources, and practice materials.

- You showed good self-discipline and motivation in your revision. You took ownership of your learning and actively sought out ways to improve your understanding.

- You effectively used feedback from teachers and peers to guide your revision and improve your understanding of the material.

- You showed good critical thinking skills in your revision. You were able to analyze complex ideas and concepts and draw meaningful conclusions.

- You demonstrated good collaboration and teamwork skills in your revision. You effectively worked with others to share knowledge and improve understanding.

- Your revision skills have improved significantly over time. Keep up the good work and continue to practice and refine your skills.

- You have shown a strong commitment to your studies and a willingness to work hard to achieve your goals. Keep up the good work and stay focused on your academic success.

CHAPTER SIXTEEN

Feedback for Class Test Performance

Here are some feedback comments that teachers could use to provide feedback to students regarding their class test performance:

- You demonstrated a good understanding of the material covered in the class test.
- Your test results showed that you had a good grasp of the concepts covered in the class.
- You were able to apply the concepts covered in the class in a thoughtful and effective way.
- You showed good attention to detail in your responses and were able to effectively communicate your ideas.
- Your test results demonstrate that you have a solid foundation in the subject matter covered in the class.
- Your test results reflect your hard work and dedication to your studies.
- You effectively used your study materials to prepare for the test, and it showed in your performance.
- You were able to work efficiently and effectively during the class test.
- Your test results show that you are making good progress in the subject matter and are well on your way to achieving your academic goals.
- You demonstrated good problem-solving skills during the test and were able to think creatively to solve complex problems.
- You showed good time management skills during the test and were able to complete all questions in the given time frame.
- Keep up the good work and continue to apply yourself to your studies to achieve even greater success in the future.

CHAPTER SEVENTEEN

Feedback for Science Test

Here are some feedback comments that teachers could use to provide feedback to students regarding their performance on a science test:

- Your understanding of the scientific concepts covered in the test is evident in your test results.
- You demonstrated good application of the scientific principles covered in the test.
- Your answers show that you have a strong grasp of the subject matter and are able to analyze and evaluate scientific data.
- You effectively used scientific terminology in your responses, which demonstrated your understanding of the material.
- Your test results indicate that you have a good foundation in the scientific concepts covered in the test.
- Your work during the test showed that you have good critical thinking skills and were able to apply them to the scientific questions.
- You were able to effectively communicate your ideas and present your answers in a clear and organized manner.
- Your test results indicate that you have made good progress in your understanding of the scientific concepts covered in the test.
- You were able to use your study materials to prepare for the test, which helped you to achieve success in the test.
- Your attention to detail in your responses shows that you have good observation skills and can analyze and interpret scientific data effectively.
- Your test results demonstrate your hard work and dedication to your studies.
- Keep up the good work and continue to apply yourself to your science studies to achieve even greater success in the future.

CHAPTER EIGHTEEN

Feedback for Math Test

Here are some feedback comments that teachers could use to provide feedback to students regarding their performance on a math test:

- Your understanding of the math concepts covered in the test is evident in your test results.
- You demonstrated good application of the math principles covered in the test.
- Your answers show that you have a strong grasp of the subject matter and are able to solve math problems accurately.
- You effectively used math terminology in your responses, which demonstrated your understanding of the material.
- Your test results indicate that you have a good foundation in the math concepts covered in the test.
- Your work during the test showed that you have good problem-solving skills and were able to apply them to the math questions.
- You were able to effectively communicate your ideas and present your answers in a clear and organized manner.
- Your test results indicate that you have made good progress in your understanding of the math concepts covered in the test.
- You were able to use your study materials to prepare for the test, which helped you to achieve success in the test.
- Your attention to detail in your responses shows that you have good observation skills and can solve math problems accurately.
- Your test results demonstrate your hard work and dedication to your studies.
- Keep up the good work and continue to apply yourself to your math studies to achieve even greater success in the future.

CHAPTER NINETEEN

Feedback for Grammar and Vocabulary

Here are some feedback comments that teachers could use to provide feedback to students regarding their grammar and vocabulary skills:

- Your writing demonstrates a strong understanding of grammar and vocabulary, which has resulted in clear and concise communication.
- You have effectively used a range of vocabulary and grammatical structures to express your ideas in a sophisticated manner.
- You have shown improvement in your grammar and vocabulary usage compared to your previous assignments.
- You have effectively applied the grammar rules and vocabulary you have learned in class to your writing.
- Your writing shows that you have a strong grasp of basic grammar and vocabulary, but could benefit from further practice and improvement in more complex structures.
- Your vocabulary usage is impressive, but your grammar needs some improvement in areas such as subject-verb agreement and sentence structure.
- You have demonstrated a good understanding of grammar and vocabulary through your participation in class discussions and the completion of homework assignments.
- Your use of varied vocabulary and grammar structures has resulted in engaging and interesting writing.
- While your grammar and vocabulary usage have improved, you still need to work on some common errors such as run-on sentences and incorrect verb tenses.
- Your writing is clear and easy to understand, but incorporating more advanced vocabulary and grammar structures will help elevate your writing to the next level.
- You have shown initiative in learning new grammar rules and vocabulary, and it is evident in your writing.
- Keep up the good work and continue to strive for excellence in your grammar and vocabulary skills!

CHAPTER TWENTY

Feedback for Spoken English

Here are some feedback comments that teachers could use to provide feedback to students regarding their spoken English skills:

- You have made excellent progress in your spoken English skills, and your communication is now clear and fluent.
- You have demonstrated confidence and poise in your spoken English, which has greatly improved your ability to express yourself.
- You have a strong grasp of grammar and vocabulary, which has enabled you to communicate your ideas effectively in English.
- Your pronunciation has improved significantly, and you are now easily understood by native English speakers.
- You have shown improvement in your ability to initiate and sustain a conversation in English, which is a key skill in language learning.
- You have effectively used a range of idiomatic expressions and phrases, which has added depth and nuance to your communication.
- Your ability to understand and respond appropriately to questions in English has improved, demonstrating your growing proficiency in the language.
- Your use of intonation and stress has improved, making your spoken English more expressive and engaging.
- You have taken initiative to practice and improve your spoken English skills outside of class, which has contributed to your progress.
- You still have room for improvement in certain areas such as reducing the use of fillers (e.g. "um," "ah") and refining your accent, but your progress is commendable.
- Keep up the good work and continue to practice your spoken English skills! Your efforts will pay off in the long run.

CHAPTER TWENTY-ONE

Feedback for Communication Skills

Here are some feedback comments that teachers could use to provide feedback to students regarding their communication skills:

- You have made excellent progress in your communication skills, and you are now able to express yourself clearly and confidently.
- Your ability to listen actively and respond appropriately to others has improved, which is a key component of effective communication.
- You have shown a willingness to share your ideas and perspectives with others, and you have done so in a respectful and considerate manner.
- You have demonstrated the ability to collaborate effectively with others, which has contributed to a positive learning environment.
- Your nonverbal communication skills, such as eye contact and body language, have improved, making you a more engaging communicator.
- You have effectively used a variety of communication modes, such as written, verbal, and digital, to convey your message.
- Your ability to adapt your communication style to different audiences and situations has improved, demonstrating your flexibility as a communicator.
- You have shown improvement in your ability to ask questions and seek clarification, which is an important aspect of effective communication.
- Your use of feedback and reflection to improve your communication skills has been commendable, demonstrating a growth mindset.
- You still have room for improvement in certain areas, such as reducing the use of filler words (e.g. "um," "like") and refining your tone and delivery, but your progress is commendable.
- Keep up the good work and continue to practice your communication skills! Effective communication is a valuable skill that will serve you well in all areas of your life.

CHAPTER TWENTY-TWO

Feedback for Games and Sports

Here are some feedback comments that teachers could use to provide feedback to students regarding their performance in games and sports:

- Your commitment and dedication to improving your skills in games and sports have been impressive.
- You have demonstrated excellent sportsmanship and teamwork, making you a valuable team player.
- Your focus and determination during practice and games have paid off, resulting in significant improvement in your performance.
- You have shown a positive attitude towards challenges and setbacks, using them as opportunities to learn and grow.
- You have consistently demonstrated excellent effort and energy during games and practices, making you an asset to the team.
- Your communication skills during games and practices have been excellent, helping the team to work together more effectively.
- You have shown an understanding of the rules and strategies of different games and sports, which has helped you to make better decisions during play.
- You have been proactive in seeking feedback and using it to improve your performance.
- Your dedication to maintaining your physical fitness and health has contributed to your success in games and sports.
- Your willingness to try new positions and take on different roles within the team has shown your adaptability and versatility.
- You still have room for improvement in certain areas, such as refining your technique and working on specific skills, but your progress is commendable.
- Keep up the good work and continue to practice your skills in games and sports! You are developing important life skills such as resilience, teamwork, and perseverance.

CHAPTER TWENTY-THREE

Feedback for Reading Skills (DEAR Club)

Here are some feedback comments that teachers could use to provide feedback to students regarding their reading skills:

- Your reading fluency has improved significantly, making it easier for you to comprehend longer and more complex texts.
- Your ability to decode words accurately and quickly has improved, making reading less frustrating and more enjoyable for you.
- Your comprehension skills have improved, allowing you to better understand what you are reading and make connections to your own experiences and prior knowledge.
- You have shown an interest in exploring different genres of literature and reading materials, which has helped to broaden your vocabulary and increase your reading skills.
- Your ability to ask thoughtful and insightful questions about what you are reading demonstrates your critical thinking skills.
- You have shown an appreciation for reading as a valuable source of information and a way to broaden your knowledge and understanding of the world.
- Your use of reading strategies, such as summarizing, making predictions, and visualizing, has helped you to engage with the text and understand it more deeply.
- You have demonstrated an ability to make connections between different texts and to draw conclusions based on evidence from the text.
- Your confidence in reading aloud and sharing your ideas with others has grown, demonstrating your growing comfort with using reading as a means of communication.
- Keep up the good work! Reading is a skill that will serve you well throughout your life, and your dedication to improving your reading skills will pay off in the long run.

CHAPTER TWENTY-FOUR

Feedback for Comprehension Skills

Here are some feedback comments that teachers could use to provide feedback to students regarding their comprehension skills:

- You have demonstrated a strong ability to identify the main idea of a text and to summarize the key points.
- Your ability to make inferences and draw conclusions based on evidence from the text has improved significantly.
- Your use of text features, such as headings, subheadings, and captions, to help you understand the structure and content of the text is impressive.
- Your ability to identify and analyze the author's purpose and point of view has improved, demonstrating a deeper understanding of the text.
- You have shown an ability to make connections between different texts and to apply what you have learned to real-life situations.
- Your use of context clues to determine the meaning of unfamiliar words is improving, making it easier for you to comprehend more challenging texts.
- You have demonstrated a growing ability to ask thoughtful questions about what you are reading and to use evidence from the text to support your answers.
- Your ability to identify and analyze literary devices, such as foreshadowing, symbolism, and irony, has improved, demonstrating a deeper understanding of the text.
- Your use of visualization and other comprehension strategies to help you understand the text is impressive.
- Keep up the good work! Your dedication to improving your comprehension skills will pay off in the long run, and you will be well-equipped to tackle more challenging texts in the future.

CHAPTER TWENTY-FIVE

Feedback for Writing Skills

Here are some feedback comments that teachers could use to provide feedback to students regarding their writing skills:

- Your writing has improved significantly, and you are demonstrating greater fluency and confidence in your expression.
- Your ability to organize your ideas and structure your writing effectively has improved, making your writing more coherent and easy to follow.
- You are making more effective use of descriptive language, which is helping to bring your writing to life and make it more engaging for the reader.
- Your use of punctuation and grammar is improving, which is helping to make your writing more clear and more precise.
- Your ability to write for different purposes and audiences is impressive, demonstrating flexibility and adaptability in your writing skills.
- Your use of evidence and examples to support your arguments and ideas is becoming more sophisticated, demonstrating a deeper understanding of the topic at hand.
- Your writing is becoming more concise and focused, which is helping to sharpen your ideas and make your arguments more persuasive.
- You are making good use of feedback to improve your writing, and your ability to revise and edit your work is helping to refine your writing skills even further.
- You have demonstrated an ability to be creative and imaginative in your writing, producing work that is both unique and compelling.
- Keep up the good work! Your dedication to improving your writing skills will pay off in the long run, and you will be well-equipped to communicate effectively in a variety of contexts.
- Here are some feedback comments that teachers could use to provide feedback to students regarding their handwriting skills:
- Your handwriting is becoming more legible and consistent, making it easier for others to read and understand your work.

- Your use of proper letter formation and spacing is improving, which is helping to make your writing more organized and professional-looking.

- Your handwriting speed is increasing, allowing you to complete written work more efficiently and effectively.

- Your ability to write in different styles and sizes is impressive, demonstrating a flexibility and adaptability in your handwriting skills.

- Your use of cursive writing is improving, which is helping to enhance the elegance and fluidity of your handwriting.

- You are making good use of feedback to improve your handwriting, and your willingness to practice and refine your skills is helping to make your writing more polished and refined.

- Your attention to detail is impressive, and you are making an effort to write neatly and carefully.

- Your handwriting is beginning to reflect your personality, and you are developing a unique and distinctive style of writing.

- Keep up the good work! Your commitment to improving your handwriting skills will pay off in the long run, and you will be well-equipped to communicate effectively through written language.

CHAPTER TWENTY-SIX

Feedback for Teamwork and Collaboration

Here are some feedback comments that teachers could use to provide feedback to students regarding their teamwork and collaboration skills:

- You demonstrate a positive attitude towards group work, and you actively engage with your teammates to accomplish the task at hand.
- You are a great listener, and you make an effort to understand your teammates' ideas and perspectives, which helps to create a collaborative environment.
- You consistently contribute to the group's discussions and activities, and you are not afraid to share your own ideas and opinions.
- Your ability to communicate effectively with your teammates is impressive, and you make an effort to clarify your own ideas and understand others' viewpoints.
- You show a willingness to compromise and negotiate with your teammates when necessary, which is an important aspect of successful collaboration.
- You are respectful of others' contributions and viewpoints, and you create a safe and inclusive environment for everyone to participate in.
- You demonstrate leadership skills by helping to guide and motivate your team toward achieving its goals.
- You are proactive in seeking feedback from your teammates, and you use this feedback to improve your own performance and contribute more effectively to the group.
- You take responsibility for your own role within the team, and you are accountable for meeting the expectations and deadlines that have been set.
- Your ability to work collaboratively with others is an important skill that will serve you well in future academic and professional endeavors. Keep up the good work!

CHAPTER TWENTY-SEVEN

Feedback for Listening Skills

Here are some feedback comments that teachers could use to provide feedback to students regarding their listening skills:

- You show great attentiveness when listening to instructions, and you make an effort to clarify any points that are unclear.
- You are respectful of others' contributions and viewpoints, and you demonstrate this by actively listening to what they have to say.
- Your ability to ask relevant questions shows that you are actively listening and engaged in the conversation.
- You are able to summarize what you have heard in your own words, which demonstrates a strong understanding of the material.
- Your body language and eye contact show that you are fully engaged in the conversation and focused on what is being said.
- You make an effort to give the speaker your undivided attention, and you avoid distractions that might interfere with your ability to listen.
- You are able to listen for key points and identify important information, which helps you to retain and understand the material.
- Your willingness to listen to and consider different perspectives is an important skill that will serve you well in future academic and professional endeavors.
- You are able to ask follow-up questions that demonstrate your understanding of the material, which shows that you are actively listening and engaged.
- Your ability to listen effectively is an important skill that will benefit you in all aspects of your life, and I encourage you to continue to develop and refine this skill.

CHAPTER TWENTY-EIGHT

Feedback for Show and Tell

Here are some feedback comments that teachers could use to provide feedback to students regarding their show and tell presentations:

- You showed great confidence and enthusiasm when presenting your show and tell, and you engaged the audience with your topic.
- Your show and tell presentation was organized and well-prepared, and you effectively conveyed your message to the audience.
- You demonstrated creativity and originality in your choice of show and tell topic, which made your presentation interesting and engaging.
- Your use of visual aids, such as props or pictures, helped to reinforce your message and made your presentation more engaging.
- You spoke clearly and audibly, and your body language and eye contact showed that you were confident and engaged with the audience.
- You effectively answered questions from the audience, demonstrating a strong understanding of your topic.
- Your show and tell presentation showed that you put a lot of thought and effort into preparing, and you should be proud of your work.
- You successfully conveyed your message in a way that was clear and engaging, and your presentation showed your creativity and originality.
- Your show and tell presentation was an excellent opportunity for you to practice your public speaking skills, and you did a great job of engaging the audience and conveying your message.
- Your show and tell presentation was a great success, and I encourage you to continue to develop your public speaking skills and share your ideas and interests with others.

CHAPTER TWENTY-NINE

Feedback for Psychomotor Skills

Here are some feedback comments that teachers could use to provide feedback to students regarding their psychomotor skills:

- You have shown significant improvement in your psychomotor skills, and your ability to perform specific tasks has greatly improved.
- Your coordination and balance have improved since we started practicing these psychomotor skills, and you are now able to complete tasks with greater ease.
- You have been practicing your psychomotor skills consistently, and it shows in the quality of your performance.
- Your attention to detail when performing psychomotor skills is impressive, and it has led to you achieving high levels of accuracy and precision.
- You are able to apply the knowledge and skills that you have learned to new and challenging situations, which is an excellent reflection of your psychomotor abilities.
- Your practice and effort in improving your psychomotor skills have paid off, and you have been able to perform more advanced techniques with ease.
- Your consistency and focus during practice have helped you develop better control and precision in your movements.
- Your commitment to mastering these psychomotor skills has been impressive, and you have shown resilience in overcoming challenges.
- You have demonstrated an ability to apply psychomotor skills in real-life situations, showing that you have a good understanding of the concepts and techniques.
- Your enthusiasm and positive attitude toward learning new psychomotor skills have been inspiring, and your progress is a testament to your hard work and dedication.

CHAPTER THIRTY

Feedback for Affective Domain

The affective domain refers to the emotional and social aspects of learning. Here are some feedback comments for students in the affective domain:

- I am so proud of how you have been showing empathy toward your classmates. Keep it up!
- You have been taking responsibility for your actions and showing great self-control. Well done!
- Your positive attitude and willingness to help others are truly inspiring.
- I have noticed how you have been actively listening to your peers and showing genuine interest in their ideas. This is a valuable skill to have.
- Your kindness and generosity towards others have not gone unnoticed. Keep spreading positivity wherever you go.
- You have been taking risks and stepping outside of your comfort zone, which shows great courage and determination.
- Your perseverance and resilience in the face of challenges is truly admirable.
- I have noticed how you have been expressing yourself confidently and respectfully during class discussions.
- Your ability to work collaboratively and respectfully with others is a valuable asset that will serve you well in the future.
- You have been demonstrating great maturity and responsibility, and I am proud of the progress you have made in the affective domain.

CHAPTER THIRTY-ONE

Feedback for Cognitive Skills

Cognitive skills refer to the mental processes used for acquiring, processing, and applying knowledge. Here are some feedback comments for students in the cognitive domain:

- Your critical thinking skills are impressive, and I have noticed how you have been able to analyze information and come up with creative solutions to problems.
- You have been demonstrating a strong understanding of complex concepts and are able to apply this knowledge in a variety of situations.
- Your attention to detail and accuracy are commendable, and I appreciate the effort you put into ensuring your work is of a high standard.
- Your ability to make connections between different concepts and ideas is a valuable skill that will serve you well in future learning.
- You have been demonstrating great curiosity and enthusiasm for learning new things, which is a wonderful quality to have.
- Your ability to organize and structure your thoughts in a clear and concise manner is a valuable skill that will help you succeed in many areas.
- You have been able to process and remember large amounts of information, which is a sign of excellent memory skills.
- Your ability to ask insightful questions and engage in meaningful discussions shows that you are actively thinking about the material we are covering in class.
- I have noticed how you have been using a variety of strategies to problem-solving and approach new challenges, which is a sign of strong cognitive flexibility.
- Your ability to learn from mistakes and adjust your approach accordingly shows great resilience and a growth mindset.

CHAPTER THIRTY-TWO

Feedback for Life skills

Here are some sample feedback comments for life skills for students:

- You showed great responsibility by taking charge of the class project and completing it on time.
- Your ability to manage your time effectively while balancing your school work and extracurricular activities is commendable.
- You have consistently shown respect towards your peers and teachers, creating a positive learning environment in the classroom.
- Your perseverance and determination in completing challenging assignments have been impressive.
- Your ability to communicate clearly and effectively with your classmates during group projects is a great strength.
- You demonstrated excellent problem-solving skills when you tackled the difficult questions on the math exam.
- Your willingness to help others and collaborate on group assignments shows great teamwork skills.
- Your resilience in the face of setbacks and obstacles is inspiring.
- Your ability to set goals and work towards achieving them is an important life skill that will serve you well in the future.
- Your positive attitude towards learning and your willingness to take on new challenges are great examples of a growth mindset.
- You consistently display kindness towards your classmates and are always willing to lend a helping hand.
- Your commitment to honesty and integrity is admirable and sets a great example for your peers.
- Your ability to show empathy towards others is a wonderful trait that fosters a positive and supportive classroom environment.
- You demonstrate excellent leadership skills by motivating and inspiring your classmates during group projects.
- Your willingness to take responsibility for your actions and learn from your mistakes shows great maturity.
- You consistently show respect towards others, regardless of differences in opinion or background.

- Your ability to collaborate with others and work towards a common goal is a valuable life skill that will serve you well in the future.
- You display excellent critical thinking skills, often challenging assumptions and seeking out new perspectives.
- Your positive attitude towards learning and your openness to trying new things is a valuable life skill that will serve you well in the future.
- You consistently show a strong work ethic and a willingness to put in extra effort to achieve your goals.

CHAPTER THIRTY-THREE

Comprehensive Feedback for Adolescents

Feedback for adolescents can be based on a variety of areas, including academic performance, social and emotional development, and personal growth. Some possible feedback comments for adolescents could include:

Academic Performance:

- You have shown excellent growth in your academic skills this year. Keep up the good work!
- I am impressed with your dedication to your studies. Your hard work is really paying off.
- You have struggled with this subject in the past, but you are making significant progress. Keep pushing yourself to learn and grow.
- I see that you have been putting a lot of effort into your homework and assignments. Keep this up and you will continue to see improvements in your grades.

Social and Emotional Development:

- You are a kind and compassionate person who is always willing to help others. Keep being a positive influence on those around you.
- I appreciate your willingness to share your thoughts and feelings with me. It takes courage to be vulnerable and open up to others.
- You have shown a lot of maturity in the way you handle conflicts and difficult situations. I am proud of you for this.
- I have noticed that you seem to be struggling lately. Please know that I am here to support you and help you through any challenges you may be facing.

Personal Growth:

- I am proud of the progress you have made in setting and achieving your personal goals. Keep up the good work!
- You have shown a lot of resilience in the face of adversity. This is an important skill that will serve you well throughout your life.
- I appreciate your willingness to try new things and step out of your comfort zone. This is a sign of bravery and growth.
- I see that you have been working on improving your time management and organization skills. This is a great step towards becoming more independent and self-sufficient.

CHAPTER THIRTY-FOUR

Comprehensive Feedback for Kindergarteners

Here are some examples of comprehensive feedback that can be given to kindergartners:

- Great job! You have made so much progress in learning the alphabet and recognizing letters. Keep practicing and soon you'll be able to read!
- Your drawings are amazing! I can see that you have a great imagination and are able to express your ideas well.
- You did a fantastic job sharing with your friends today. You listened carefully to what they had to say and responded kindly. Well done!
- Your counting skills are really coming along. Keep practicing and soon you'll be able to count all the way to 100!
- You did a great job following directions during our activity today. You listened carefully and did exactly what was asked of you. Keep up the good work!
- Your handwriting is looking much better than last time. You are holding your pencil correctly and forming your letters well. Keep practicing and your handwriting will get even better.
- I am so proud of how you are showing kindness and respect to your classmates. You are being a great friend and a positive role model.
- Your enthusiasm for learning is contagious! I can see how much you enjoy coming to school and trying new things. Keep up the great attitude!
- You are doing a wonderful job taking turns and sharing toys during playtime. You are showing great social skills and consideration for others.
- Your participation in class discussions is excellent. You are asking thoughtful questions and sharing your ideas with the group. Keep up the great contributions!

CHAPTER THIRTY-FIVE

Feedback for Formative Assessments

Formative assessment feedback is an essential component of the learning process, which enables students to identify their strengths and weaknesses and improve their learning outcomes. Here are some examples of formative assessment feedback for students:

Strengths:

- You demonstrated a strong understanding of the key concepts covered in this unit.
- You were able to apply your knowledge to solve complex problems effectively.
- You showed good analytical and critical thinking skills in your responses.

Areas for improvement:

- You need to work on your time management skills to ensure that you complete tasks within the given time frame.
- You should focus on improving your writing skills, especially in terms of grammar and sentence structure.
- You need to pay more attention to the details of the instructions to avoid making careless errors.

Suggestions for improvement:

- Try to use more examples and evidence to support your arguments in your responses.
- Take some time to review your notes and other resources to ensure that you have a clear understanding of the concepts covered in the class.
- Consider working with a study group or a tutor to help you identify and address your areas of weakness.
- Remember, the purpose of formative assessment feedback is to provide students with the guidance and support they need to improve their learning outcomes. Encourage them to take the feedback positively and work on the areas identified to enhance their overall performance.

CHAPTER THIRTY-SIX

Feedback for Routine Assessments

Here are some class assessment comments that teachers can provide to their students:

- Your active participation in class discussions has been impressive. Keep it up!
- You have demonstrated a strong grasp of the concepts taught in this class. Good job!
- You have made great progress in this class. Keep striving for excellence!
- You have been struggling in some areas, but your effort to improve is evident. Keep working hard!
- Your ability to work collaboratively with your classmates is commendable.
- Your consistent submission of homework and class assignments is impressive.
- Your enthusiasm for learning is inspiring. Keep up the positive attitude!
- You have been making an effort to ask questions and seek clarification, which shows a desire to learn.
- Your class behavior and punctuality have been excellent. Keep up the good work!
- You have made a significant improvement in your performance since the beginning of the class. Keep up the momentum!
- Great job on this class test! Your hard work and effort paid off with an excellent grade.
- You have a good understanding of the material, but be sure to pay attention to the details and take your time when answering questions.
- You struggled with some of the concepts on this test. Consider scheduling some extra study time and reviewing the material with your teacher.
- Your answers were well-organized and demonstrated a clear understanding of the material. Keep up the good work!
- You made a few careless mistakes on this test. Be sure to double-check your work before turning it in.
- You seem to have a good grasp on the concepts, but try to apply them more effectively in your responses.

- Keep up the good work, but don't forget to challenge yourself and strive for even better results in the future.
- You demonstrated a good understanding of the material, but be sure to work on your time management and pacing during the test.
- Your answers showed a clear understanding of the material, but consider going beyond the basic concepts and delving deeper into the subject matter.
- You may benefit from more practice and review on this topic before moving on to the next lesson. Don't hesitate to ask for extra help if needed.

CHAPTER THIRTY-SEVEN

Feedback for Physics Students

Here are some sample feedback comments for students in a physics class:

- "Great job on your lab report! You demonstrated a clear understanding of the concepts and followed the procedures accurately."
- "Your problem-solving skills are impressive. Keep up the good work!"
- "I noticed that you struggled with the topic we covered in class today. Let's schedule some extra time for one-on-one instruction."
- "Your class participation is lacking. Please make an effort to contribute to discussions and ask questions."
- "You have a talent for explaining complex ideas in simple terms. Consider helping your classmates who may be struggling with the material."
- "I appreciate your attention to detail in your work. Just be sure to double-check your calculations before submitting your assignments."
- "You seem to be having difficulty with the math involved in these physics problems. Let's review some basic algebra together."
- "I enjoyed reading your research paper. Your writing is clear and concise, and you incorporated a variety of reliable sources."
- "Your presentation skills are improving, but remember to speak clearly and confidently, and use visuals to support your points."
- "You demonstrated excellent critical thinking skills in your response to the prompt. Keep up the good work!"

CHAPTER THIRTY-EIGHT

Feedback for Chemistry Students

Here are some feedback comments for students in chemistry:

- You have shown great interest in learning the concepts of chemistry. Keep up the good work!
- Your lab reports have been detailed and well-organized. Keep working on your practical skills.
- You seem to struggle with some of the more complex chemical equations. Try to break them down into smaller parts and practice them regularly.
- Your participation in class discussions and group activities has been excellent. Keep up the active involvement in the learning process.
- Your knowledge of the periodic table is impressive. Keep expanding your knowledge by learning about the properties and reactions of different elements.
- You have demonstrated good analytical skills in solving chemical problems. Keep practicing and refining your problem-solving techniques.
- You have shown improvement in your accuracy in conducting experiments. Keep working on refining your techniques to improve your precision.
- Your curiosity and eagerness to learn about the applications of chemistry in the real world is commendable. Keep exploring and learning more about the practical uses of chemistry in our lives.
- Your understanding of the different types of chemical reactions is impressive. Keep practicing and identifying them in various chemical scenarios.
- You need to work on improving your memorization of chemical formulas and equations. Practice with flashcards and repetition to improve your retention of the material.

CHAPTER THIRTY-NINE

Feedback for Biology Students

Here are some feedback comments for biology students:

- You showed a good understanding of the key biological concepts we covered in class.
- You demonstrated a strong ability to apply the scientific method during our lab experiments.
- Your attention to detail during dissection was impressive.
- I noticed a significant improvement in your ability to memorize complex biological terms and concepts.
- Your explanations of biological phenomena were clear and concise.
- You had excellent participation during class discussions, and your questions showed a high level of critical thinking.
- I appreciate your effort to connect class topics to real-world examples.
- Your ability to draw accurate and detailed diagrams helped to reinforce your understanding of biological processes.
- You showed a great deal of curiosity and interest in learning about different biological topics.
- Your lab reports were well-written and demonstrated a strong understanding of scientific writing conventions.

CHAPTER FORTY

Feedback for Science Diagrams

Here are some feedback comments for science diagrams:

- Your diagram is well-drawn and clearly labeled, making it easy to understand the concepts.
- The labeling on your diagram is incomplete. Please make sure to label all relevant parts of the diagram.
- Your diagram could be improved with the addition of color and shading to make it more visually appealing and easier to understand.
- You have included too much detail in your diagram, making it difficult to see the main idea. Please simplify the diagram and focus on the most important parts.
- Your diagram is missing key elements that are necessary to understand the concept. Please review the instructions and make sure to include all required elements.
- You have done a great job on your diagram. I appreciate the effort you put into creating a clear and accurate representation of the scientific concept.

CHAPTER FORTY-ONE

Feedback for PowerPoint Presentations

Feedback for a PowerPoint presentation may include the following:

Organization: Comment on how well the presentation was structured and whether the main points were presented in a clear and logical manner.

Visuals: Evaluate the use of visual aids such as images, graphs, and charts. Did they enhance the presentation or detract from it?

Clarity: Evaluate the speaker's clarity of speech, the quality of the microphone and the sound system.

Engagement: Comment on whether the presentation was engaging and kept the audience interested. Were there any parts where the audience seemed to lose interest?

Content: Evaluate the accuracy and relevance of the information presented.

Delivery: Comment on the speaker's tone of voice, eye contact, and body language. Did the presenter engage with the audience?

Time Management: Evaluate whether the presentation was delivered within the allotted time frame.

Overall Impression: Summarize your overall impression of the presentation and offer suggestions for improvement.

Example: "Great job on your PowerPoint presentation! The content was relevant and accurate, and the visuals were well-chosen and helped to reinforce the main points. You spoke clearly and had good eye contact with the audience. It would have been helpful to spend more time on the conclusion and less on the introduction, and perhaps incorporate more interactive elements to engage the audience. Overall, well done!"

CHAPTER FORTY-TWO

Feedback for Kindergarten Students on Graduation Day

- Congratulations, Kindergarten graduates! You have completed an important milestone in your educational journey, and we are so proud of you! You have learned so much this year, and it's been amazing to see how much you have grown and developed.
- Your enthusiasm and curiosity have been a joy to witness, and you have shown great determination and resilience in overcoming challenges. You have made new friends, learned new skills, and explored new ideas. We know that you will continue to learn and grow as you move forward in your education.
- Remember to keep dreaming big and setting goals for yourself. Always believe in yourself and never give up on your dreams. We wish you all the best as you enter a new chapter in your lives. Congratulations once again, and we can't wait to see what you will accomplish in the future!

CHAPTER FORTY-THREE

Feedback for Subject Concept Clarity

Here are some feedback comments for subject-related concept clarity for students:

- "You have demonstrated a clear understanding of the fundamental concepts in [subject]. Keep up the good work!"
- "Your explanations of [subject] concepts are concise and accurate. You have a great grasp of the material."
- "It's evident that you've put in a lot of effort to understand the more complex concepts in [subject]. Keep asking questions and seeking clarification when needed."
- "I'm impressed by your ability to break down the more challenging topics in [subject]. Your understanding of the material is excellent."
- "Your grasp of [subject] concepts has noticeably improved since the start of the term. Keep practicing and seeking feedback to continue making progress."
- "You've demonstrated a good understanding of the basics of [subject], but you may benefit from further review of the more advanced concepts."
- "I appreciate your willingness to ask questions when you're unsure about a topic in [subject]. Keep up the curiosity and dedication to learning."
- "Your hard work and persistence in studying the concepts in [subject] have paid off. Your understanding of the material is impressive."
- "It's clear that you enjoy learning about [subject], and your curiosity and enthusiasm for the material are evident in your understanding of the concepts."
- "Remember to keep practicing and reviewing the concepts in [subject] regularly to maintain and deepen your understanding."

CHAPTER FORTY-FOUR

Feedback for Technological Skills

Here are some feedback comments for students regarding their technological skills:

- You have shown good proficiency in using various digital tools and technologies.
- Your ability to adapt to new technological advancements is impressive.
- You seem to be very comfortable using computers and other digital devices.
- You have demonstrated excellent problem-solving skills while working with technology.
- Your knowledge of various software programs and digital platforms is remarkable.
- You are quick to learn new technological skills and apply them effectively.
- Your creativity in using technology to enhance your learning experience is commendable.
- You have shown great initiative in using technology to complete your assignments.
- You are proficient in using multimedia tools to create engaging and informative projects.
- Your ability to navigate digital resources and use them effectively for research is impressive.

CHAPTER FORTY-FIVE

Feedback for Debate

Here are some feedback comments for a debate:

- "You presented your points clearly and with confidence."
- "Your rebuttals were strong and effectively countered the arguments of the opposing team."
- "You showed a good understanding of the topic and supported your arguments with solid evidence."
- "Your use of persuasive language and rhetorical devices was impressive."
- "You could work on maintaining eye contact with the audience throughout the debate."
- "You had a tendency to speak too quickly at times, which made it difficult to follow your argument."
- "You could have done more to engage with the opposing team's arguments and address any weaknesses in your own argument."
- "Your opening and closing statements were impactful and left a strong impression on the audience."
- "You demonstrated good teamwork and collaboration with your debate partner."
- "Overall, you did a great job and showed a lot of potential as a debater."

CHAPTER FORTY-SIX

Feedback for Group Discussions

Here are some feedback comments for group discussions:

- Great job leading the discussion today. You kept the conversation flowing and ensured everyone had a chance to share their ideas.
- I appreciate your active participation in today's group discussion. Your insightful comments helped move the conversation forward.
- You did a fantastic job listening to others and respectfully sharing your own thoughts during our group discussion. Keep it up!
- I noticed that you really made an effort to involve everyone in the conversation today. That kind of inclusivity is a great example for others to follow.
- Your ability to build on the ideas of others and connect them to the overall topic of discussion was impressive today.
- Your open-mindedness and willingness to consider different perspectives really contributed to the success of our group discussion.
- It was great to see you taking initiative and helping to guide our group discussion towards a productive outcome.
- Your preparation and thoughtful contributions really helped make our group discussion today insightful and engaging.

CHAPTER FORTY-SEVEN

Feedback for Kindergarten Report Cards

Here are some remarks that can be used for report cards for kindergarten students:

- Shows enthusiasm and curiosity for learning new things.
- Follows classroom routines and rules with ease.
- Demonstrates good listening and attention skills during lessons.
- Participates actively in class activities and discussions.
- Shows improvement in basic literacy and numeracy skills.
- Demonstrates good social skills and interacts positively with peers.
- Takes responsibility for personal belongings and belongings of others.
- Demonstrates creativity and imagination in various activities.
- Shows interest in exploring and discovering new things.
- Is developing good problem-solving and critical thinking skills.
- Is developing good motor skills, both fine and gross.
- Demonstrates good hygiene habits and takes care of personal needs independently.
- Shows respect for adults and peers.
- Is able to work independently and in groups.
- Is developing good communication skills and expressing oneself effectively.
- Remember to provide specific examples to support the remarks and to use positive language to encourage the child's growth and development.

CHAPTER FORTY-EIGHT

Feedback for Primary School Report Cards

Here are some remarks that can be used for report cards for primary students:

- Shows a positive attitude towards learning and takes initiative in classroom activities.
- Demonstrates good listening and comprehension skills during lessons.
- Participates actively in class discussions and contributes thoughtful ideas.
- Demonstrates good problem-solving and critical thinking skills.
- Shows improvement in reading, writing, and math skills.
- Is able to work independently and in groups.
- Shows respect for adults and peers and interacts positively with them.
- Is developing good study habits and is organized with their assignments and materials.
- Takes responsibility for their learning and seeks help when needed.
- Demonstrates creativity and imagination in various activities.
- Is developing good time management skills and completes tasks within deadlines.
- Shows good sportsmanship and participates actively in physical education.
- Is able to use technology appropriately and responsibly.
- Shows an interest in learning about different cultures and perspectives.
- Is developing good communication skills and expressing oneself effectively.
- Remember to provide specific examples to support the remarks and to use positive language to encourage the child's growth and development. It's important to acknowledge both their strengths and areas for improvement, while also providing guidance for how they can continue to improve.

CHAPTER FORTY-NINE

Feedback for Middle School Report Cards

Here are some remarks that can be used for report cards for middle school students:

- Demonstrates good time management and organization skills.
- Takes responsibility for their learning and seeks help when needed.
- Shows an eagerness to learn and takes initiative in class.
- Demonstrates good critical thinking and problem-solving skills.
- Participates actively in class discussions and contributes thoughtful ideas.
- Shows improvement in reading, writing, and math skills.
- Is able to work independently and in groups, and demonstrates good collaboration skills.
- Demonstrates good study habits and completes assignments within deadlines.
- Shows respect for adults and peers and interacts positively with them.
- Is developing good research skills and can evaluate sources critically.
- Shows an interest in learning about different cultures and perspectives.
- Is developing good presentation skills and can communicate ideas effectively.
- Demonstrates good sportsmanship and participates actively in physical education.
- Uses technology appropriately and responsibly.
- Is developing good leadership skills and can take on responsibilities in groups.
- Remember to provide specific examples to support the remarks and to use positive language to encourage the child's growth and development. It's important to acknowledge both their strengths and areas for improvement, while also providing guidance for how they can continue to improve.

CHAPTER FIFTY

Feedback for High School Report Cards

Here are some remarks that can be used for report cards for high school students:

- Shows a strong commitment to academic success and takes initiative in their learning.
- Demonstrates critical thinking and problem-solving skills in their coursework.
- Participates actively in class discussions and contributes thoughtful ideas.
- Shows improvement in advanced reading, writing, and math skills.
- Is able to work independently and in groups, and demonstrates strong collaboration skills.
- Demonstrates good time management and organization skills, and meets deadlines consistently.
- Uses technology effectively and appropriately to support learning.
- Shows respect for adults and peers and interacts positively with them.
- Is developing good research skills and can evaluate sources critically.
- Shows an interest in learning about different cultures and perspectives.
- Is developing strong presentation skills and can communicate ideas effectively.
- Demonstrates good sportsmanship and participates actively in physical education.
- Is developing leadership skills and can take on responsibilities in groups.
- Is preparing well for college and/or career paths after graduation.
- Takes responsibility for their actions and makes positive choices for their future.
- Remember to provide specific examples to support the remarks and to use positive language to encourage the student's growth and development. It's important to acknowledge both their strengths and areas for improvement, while also providing guidance for how they can continue to improve and excel.

CHAPTER FIFTY-ONE

Feedback for Kindergarten Notebook Correction

Here are some notebook correction feedback remarks that can be used for kindergarten students:

- Great job! Your work is neat and organized.
- You are doing a great job practicing your writing skills.
- Keep up the good work on coloring within the lines.
- You are showing improvement in tracing letters and numbers.
- Nice job on following the instructions carefully.
- You are doing well in recognizing and writing your name.
- Your drawings are creative and imaginative.
- You are doing well in identifying and matching colors.
- Keep practicing your cutting skills, you are improving!
- You are showing progress in identifying shapes and patterns.
- You are doing well in following the classroom rules.
- You are showing good effort and focus on your work.
- Keep up the good work on writing and counting numbers.
- You are demonstrating good listening and concentration skills.
- You are showing improvement in identifying and writing basic sight words.

Remember to provide specific and constructive feedback that will encourage the child to improve while also highlighting their achievements. Use positive language to help build their confidence and motivate them to continue to work hard.

CHAPTER FIFTY-TWO

Feedback for Primary School Notebooks

Here are some notebook correction feedback remarks that can be used for primary school students:

- Excellent work! Your work is neat, organized, and easy to read.
- You are doing a great job practicing your handwriting and developing your own writing style.
- Keep up the good work on paying attention to spelling and grammar.
- You are showing improvement in solving math problems and explaining your thought process.
- Great job on following directions and completing assignments on time.
- Your drawings and artwork are creative and show attention to detail.
- You are showing good effort and focus on your work.
- You are doing well in identifying and using descriptive language.
- Keep practicing your reading skills, you are showing improvement!
- You are demonstrating good listening and concentration skills in class.
- Your research skills are improving, keep it up!
- You are showing progress in identifying and analyzing literary devices in texts.
- Keep up the good work on using technology appropriately to support your learning.
- You are developing good study habits and time management skills.
- You are showing good sportsmanship and team collaboration skills.

Remember to provide specific and constructive feedback that will encourage the child to improve while also highlighting their achievements. Use positive language to help build their confidence and motivate them to continue to work hard. Additionally, you can provide specific suggestions for areas that need improvement and encourage the student to take initiative in their learning.

CHAPTER FIFTY-THREE

Feedback for Middle School Notebooks

Here are some notebook correction feedback remarks that can be used for middle school students:

- Your work is well-organized and shows attention to detail.
- You are demonstrating good critical thinking skills and showing your thought process clearly.
- Keep up the good work on developing your own writing style and improving your grammar and vocabulary.
- You are showing improvement in analyzing and interpreting texts.
- Great job on completing assignments on time and following directions carefully.
- Your drawings and diagrams show creativity and a good understanding of the subject.
- You are demonstrating good research skills and can evaluate sources critically.
- You are developing good study habits and time management skills.
- Keep practicing your reading skills, you are showing progress!
- Your presentations are clear and well-structured.
- You are showing good sportsmanship and team collaboration skills.
- Your work is becoming more sophisticated and advanced.
- You are showing good effort and focus on your work.
- You are using technology effectively and appropriately to support your learning.
- Your contributions to class discussions are thoughtful and insightful.

Remember to provide specific and constructive feedback that will encourage the student to improve while also highlighting their achievements. Use positive language to help build their confidence and motivate them to continue to work hard. Additionally, you can provide specific suggestions for areas that need improvement and encourage the student to take initiative in their learning.

CHAPTER FIFTY-FOUR

Feedback for High School Notebooks

Here are some notebook correction feedback remarks that can be used for high school students:

- Your work is well-organized, and detailed, and shows a strong understanding of the subject.
- You are demonstrating excellent critical thinking and analytical skills.
- Keep up the good work on developing your own writing style and using complex sentence structures.
- You are showing excellent research skills and can evaluate sources critically.
- Great job on completing assignments on time and following instructions carefully.
- Your presentations are clear, and engaging, and demonstrate a strong grasp of the material.
- You are demonstrating good study habits and time management skills.
- Keep practicing your reading skills, you are showing progress!
- Your work shows a high level of sophistication and originality.
- Your contributions to class discussions are thoughtful and insightful and demonstrate a strong command of the subject matter.
- You are demonstrating good sportsmanship and team collaboration skills.
- Your use of technology is effective and appropriate and enhances your learning experience.
- You are showing excellent effort and focus on your work.
- You are demonstrating good leadership skills and can take on responsibilities in groups.
- Your work is of a consistently high standard and demonstrates a commitment to academic excellence.

Remember to provide specific and constructive feedback that will encourage the student to improve while also highlighting their achievements. Use positive language to help build their confidence and motivate them to continue to work hard. Additionally, you can provide specific suggestions for areas that need improvement and encourage the student to take initiative in their learning.

CHAPTER FIFTY-FIVE

Comprehensive Feedback for Languages (English/ Hindi/ Punjabi...any languages)

Reading: [Student's name] has made great progress in reading this year. They have developed strong decoding skills and are beginning to read with greater fluency. However, they could benefit from additional practice with comprehension strategies to better understand what they are reading.

Writing: [Student's name] has shown a lot of creativity in their writing this year. They use descriptive language to bring their stories to life and are starting to use more complex sentence structures. However, they could work on improving their spelling and punctuation to make their writing more polished.

Speaking and Listening: [Student's name] is an active participant in class discussions and listens attentively to their classmates. They are able to express their ideas clearly and respectfully, and they show good listening skills by asking questions and responding to others.

Grammar and Vocabulary: [Student's name] has a solid understanding of basic grammar and vocabulary concepts. They use correct verb tenses and subject-verb agreement in their writing and speech. However, they could benefit from expanding their vocabulary to use more sophisticated words and phrases.

Overall Language Skills: [Student's name] has shown steady progress in their English skills this year. They have a positive attitude toward learning and are eager to improve. With continued effort and practice, they have the potential to excel in this subject.

CHAPTER FIFTY-SIX

Comprehensive Feedback for Mathematics

Number Sense: [Student's name] has shown great progress in developing their number sense this year. They can count, compare and order numbers with ease, and can apply their understanding of place value to solve problems. However, they could benefit from additional practice with more complex operations such as multiplication and division.

Problem-Solving: [Student's name] is a skilled problem solver who can use a variety of strategies to find solutions. They are able to identify the relevant information in a problem and apply their mathematical understanding to arrive at a solution. However, they could benefit from additional practice with real-world problems that require critical thinking and creativity.

Measurement: [Student's name] has a good understanding of units of measurement and can convert between them with ease. They are able to estimate and measure lengths, weights, and volumes accurately. However, they could benefit from additional practice with more complex measurements such as time, temperature, and angles.

Geometry: [Student's name] has shown great progress in their understanding of shapes and their properties. They can identify and classify two-dimensional and three-dimensional shapes with ease, and can use their understanding of symmetry to create and identify patterns. However, they could benefit from additional practice with more complex concepts such as angles and transformations.

Overall Math Skills: [Student's name] has shown steady progress in their math skills this year. They have a positive attitude toward learning and are eager to improve. With continued effort and practice, they have the potential to excel in this subject.

CHAPTER FIFTY-SEVEN

Comprehensive Feedback for Science

Scientific Inquiry: [Student's name] has shown great progress in their ability to ask questions, make observations, and gather data. They can conduct simple experiments and draw conclusions based on their findings. However, they could benefit from additional practice with making and recording observations accurately.

Life Science: [Student's name] has a good understanding of basic life science concepts, including the characteristics of living things, the life cycles of plants and animals, and the basic needs of living things. However, they could benefit from additional practice with more complex concepts such as adaptations, ecosystems and food chains.

Physical Science: [Student's name] has shown progress in their understanding of basic physical science concepts, including properties of matter, simple machines, and energy. However, they could benefit from additional practice with more complex concepts such as forces, motion, and the relationship between heat and temperature.

Earth Science: [Student's name] has a good understanding of basic Earth science concepts, including the water cycle, rocks and minerals, and basic weather patterns. However, they could benefit from additional practice with more complex concepts such as the causes of natural disasters, Earth's structure, and the impact of human activities on the environment.

Overall Science Skills: [Student's name] has shown steady progress in their science skills this year. They have a positive attitude toward learning and are eager to improve. With continued effort and practice, they have the potential to excel in this subject.

When writing remarks for primary students in social science, it's important to keep in mind their age and level of understanding about society and the world.

CHAPTER FIFTY-EIGHT

Comprehensive Feedback for Social Science

Here are some examples of social science subject remarks you might write:

Geography: [Student's name] has shown good progress in their understanding of basic geography concepts, including maps, directions, and continents. They are able to locate different countries and continents and identify their unique features. However, they could benefit from additional practice with more complex concepts such as climate, landforms, and the impact of human activities on the environment.

History: [Student's name] has shown progress in their understanding of historical events and concepts, including important people and events in their own country and around the world. They are able to draw conclusions and make connections between different historical events. However, they could benefit from additional practice in analyzing and interpreting historical sources and understanding cause and effect.

Civics/ Political Science: [Student's name] has a good understanding of basic civics concepts, including the rights and responsibilities of citizens, democracy, and government. They are able to identify and describe different forms of government and their functions. However, they could benefit from additional practice in understanding how government policies and decisions impact individuals and communities.

Economics: [Student's name] has shown progress in their understanding of basic economics concepts, including goods and services, needs and wants, and supply and demand. They are able to identify and explain different economic systems and the factors that affect the economy. However, they could benefit from additional practice in understanding money management and the impact of financial decisions on individuals and society.

Overall Social Science Skills: [Student's name] has shown steady progress in their social science skills this year. They have a positive attitude towards learning and are eager to improve. With continued effort and practice, they have the potential to excel in this subject.

CHAPTER FIFTY-NINE

Feedback for Kindergarten Activities

When writing activity participation remarks for primary students, it's important to acknowledge the child's individual strengths and areas for improvement. Here are some examples of activity participation remarks you might write:

Sports: [Student's name] has shown great enthusiasm and dedication when participating in sports. They demonstrate good sportsmanship and team spirit. They could benefit from additional practice to improve their skills in specific areas.

Music: [Student's name] has shown a natural talent for music and enjoys participating in various musical activities. They demonstrate good focus and attention during rehearsals and performances. They could benefit from additional practice to improve their technical skills.

Art: [Student's name] has shown a strong interest in art and enjoys expressing creativity through various mediums. They are able to follow instructions well and take pride in their work. They could benefit from additional practice to improve their attention to detail and their ability to communicate their artistic vision.

Drama: [Student's name] has shown a natural flair for drama and enjoys participating in dramatic activities. They demonstrate good speaking skills and have a good stage presence. They could benefit from additional practice to improve their ability to interpret and communicate different characters.

Overall Activity Participation: [Student's name] has shown enthusiasm and dedication when participating in various activities. They demonstrate good effort and a positive attitude towards learning new skills. With continued effort and practice, they have the potential to excel in their chosen activities.

CHAPTER SIXTY

Feedback for Primary School Activities

When writing activity participation remarks for kindergarten students, it's important to keep in mind their age and developmental level. Here are some examples of activity participation remarks you might write:

Arts and Crafts: [Student's name] enjoys participating in arts and crafts activities. They have shown good effort in following instructions and using different materials to create artwork. They could benefit from additional practice to improve their fine motor skills and attention to detail.

Music and Movement: [Student's name] has shown enthusiasm and enjoys participating in music and movement activities. They are able to follow simple rhythms and movements and enjoy singing and dancing. They could benefit from additional practice to improve their ability to follow instructions and maintain focus during group activities.

Story Time: [Student's name] enjoys listening to stories and is able to participate in group discussions about the books. They demonstrate good listening skills and are able to follow along with the story. They could benefit from additional practice to improve their ability to identify characters, settings, and plot.

Outdoor Play: [Student's name] enjoys playing outside and has shown good effort in participating in various games and activities. They are able to follow the rules of the games and work cooperatively with their peers. They could benefit from additional practice to improve their gross motor skills and coordination.

Overall Activity Participation: [Student's name] has shown enthusiasm and effort when participating in various activities. They demonstrate a positive attitude towards learning new skills and enjoy exploring different interests. With continued effort and practice, they have the potential to excel in their chosen activities.

CHAPTER SIXTY-ONE

Feedback for Senior Students

Here are some sample report card comments for senior students:

Academic Achievements:

- [Student's name] has demonstrated a high level of academic achievement throughout the year, consistently producing work of a very high standard.
- [Student's name] is an excellent student who consistently produces high-quality work, particularly in [subject area].
- [Student's name] is a dedicated and hard-working student who has achieved excellent results in all subject areas.
- [Student's name] has made significant improvements in their academic performance this year, particularly in [subject area], and should be commended for their efforts.

Work Habits:

- [Student's name] consistently demonstrates a strong work ethic and is always willing to go above and beyond to achieve their goals.
- [Student's name] is a diligent and conscientious student who always puts in their best effort, even when faced with difficult tasks.
- [Student's name] has excellent time management skills and consistently meets deadlines and completes tasks to a high standard.
- [Student's name] is an excellent collaborator and works well with their peers, contributing positively to group projects and discussions.

Behaviour:

- [Student's name] is a respectful and courteous student who is always polite and considerate of their peers and teachers.
- [Student's name] is a positive role model for their peers and demonstrates excellent leadership qualities.
- [Student's name] is a reliable and responsible student who can be counted on to follow school rules and policies.
- [Student's name] demonstrates a positive attitude towards learning and is always eager to participate in class discussions and activities.
- Areas for Improvement:
- [Student's name] could benefit from further development in [subject area], and may benefit from additional support or tutoring in this area.
- [Student's name] should work on developing their communication and interpersonal skills to improve their ability to work collaboratively with peers.
- [Student's name] could benefit from setting more specific and achievable goals to help them focus their efforts and improve their performance.

- [Student's name] should work on developing better study habits and time management skills to improve their overall academic performance.

CHAPTER SIXTY-TWO

Feedback for Art-Integrated Learning

Here are some art-integrated learning feedback comments for students:

Creativity and Imagination:

- [Student's name] has demonstrated excellent creativity and imagination in their artwork, using a range of materials and techniques to create unique and interesting pieces.
- [Student's name] has shown an impressive ability to think outside the box and come up with innovative solutions to artistic challenges.
- [Student's name] has demonstrated an excellent understanding of the creative process, and has used their imagination to explore new ideas and approaches to art.

Artistic Techniques:

- [Student's name] has shown impressive technical skills in their artwork, demonstrating proficiency in a range of materials and techniques.
- [Student's name] has shown a willingness to experiment with new materials and techniques, and has developed their skills significantly over the course of the term/year.
- [Student's name] has demonstrated a strong understanding of color theory, composition, and other key artistic principles, and has used this knowledge to create impressive works of art.

Integration with Other Subjects:

- [Student's name] has successfully integrated their learning in other subject areas, using art as a way to explore and reinforce key concepts.
- [Student's name] has demonstrated an excellent understanding of how art can be used to communicate ideas and concepts, and has successfully applied this understanding to their work in other subject areas.
- [Student's name] has shown a willingness to collaborate with peers and teachers in other subject areas, using art as a way to enhance their learning and understanding.

Reflection and Evaluation:

- [Student's name] has demonstrated an excellent ability to reflect on their artwork and evaluate their own progress and growth as an artist.
- [Student's name] has shown an impressive level of self-awareness and critical thinking, using their reflections to identify areas for improvement and set goals for future work.
- [Student's name] has demonstrated a commitment to continuous learning and improvement, and has used feedback from peers and teachers to refine their artistic skills and techniques.

CHAPTER SIXTY-THREE

Feedback for Co-curricular Activities

Here are some co-curricular activity participation comments for students:

Leadership and Initiative:

- [Student's name] has shown excellent leadership skills and has taken the initiative to organize and lead activities both inside and outside of school.
- [Student's name] has demonstrated a strong sense of responsibility and has taken on significant leadership roles in their co-curricular activities.
- [Student's name] has shown a willingness to take risks and try new things, and has been a positive influence on their peers in their co-curricular activities.

Collaboration and Teamwork:

- [Student's name] has demonstrated excellent collaboration and teamwork skills, working effectively with their peers to achieve common goals.
- [Student's name] has shown an ability to communicate effectively with others and has played an important role in fostering a positive and supportive team environment.
- [Student's name] has demonstrated a commitment to supporting their teammates and has been a positive influence on team morale and cohesion.

Skill Development:

- [Student's name] has demonstrated significant growth and improvement in their skills and abilities through their participation in co-curricular activities.
- [Student's name] has shown a willingness to learn new skills and techniques, and has made impressive progress in developing their talents and abilities.
- [Student's name] has shown an impressive level of dedication and commitment to their co-curricular activities, and has worked hard to develop their skills and achieve their goals.

Impact on Others:

- [Student's name] has had a positive impact on their peers through their participation in co-curricular activities, serving as a role model and inspiration to others.
- [Student's name] has shown a commitment to making a difference in their community through their involvement in volunteer and service projects.
- [Student's name] has demonstrated a strong sense of empathy and compassion, and has used their co-curricular activities as a way to make a positive difference in the lives of others.

CHAPTER SIXTY-FOUR

Encouraging Feedback for Students

Here are some encouragement comments for students:

- Keep up the good work! You are doing great.
- I am impressed with the effort you are putting in.
- Your hard work is paying off.
- You are showing real improvement in this subject.
- I can see that you are really committed to your studies.
- Don't give up! You are capable of achieving great things.
- Keep pushing yourself. You have so much potential.
- Your perseverance and dedication will pay off in the long run.
- I believe in you and your abilities.
- Your positive attitude and enthusiasm are infectious. Keep it up!
- Remember that mistakes are opportunities to learn and grow.
- You are making progress every day, even if it doesn't always feel like it.
- Your unique talents and skills are valuable and will take you far in life.
- Your passion and curiosity are inspiring. Keep exploring and discovering new things.
- You are capable of overcoming any challenges that come your way. Keep pushing forward!

CHAPTER SIXTY-FIVE

Notebook remarks for homework by teachers

Here are some notebook remarks for homework that teachers could use to provide feedback to students:

- Well done! Your homework is complete and well-organized.
- I can see that you put in a lot of effort on this assignment.
- You have done a great job of demonstrating your understanding of the material.
- Your work shows that you have taken the time to review and revise your answers.
- I appreciate your attention to detail and neat handwriting.
- Keep up the good work! You are making progress.
- It looks like you have struggled with some of the questions. Let's review them together.
- I can see that you have improved since the last assignment. Keep it up!
- Your answers are correct, but I would like to see more detailed explanations.
- Great start, but let's work on improving your accuracy and consistency.
- Your work shows that you are thinking critically and applying your knowledge.
- I appreciate your creativity and unique approach to the assignment.
- I can see that you have put in extra effort to complete this assignment.
- Your answers are well-reasoned and supported by evidence.
- Keep asking questions and seeking help when you need it. You are on the right track!

CHAPTER SIXTY-SIX

Revision work feedback comments

Here are some revision work feedback comments that teachers could use to provide feedback to students:

- You have done a great job revising your work. Your understanding of the material has improved significantly.
- I can see that you have taken the time to review your notes and make corrections.
- Your work shows that you have identified your weaknesses and have focused on improving them.
- Keep up the good work! Your revision efforts are paying off.
- Your revisions have helped to clarify your thinking and have made your work more coherent.
- I appreciate your attention to detail and the care you have taken in revising your work.
- Your revisions have helped to strengthen your arguments and make them more convincing.
- I can see that you have put in a lot of effort to improve your work. It shows!
- Your revisions have made your work more accurate and have helped to eliminate errors.
- Great job identifying the areas that needed improvement and working to make them better.
- Your revisions have helped to add depth and complexity to your work.
- Keep reviewing and refining your work. You are on the right track!
- Your revisions have helped to demonstrate your mastery of the material.
- I appreciate the time and effort you have put into revising your work. It has made a noticeable difference.
- Your revisions have helped to make your work more engaging and enjoyable to read.

CHAPTER SIXTY-SEVEN

Literature work feedback for students

Here are some literature work feedback comments that teachers could use to provide feedback to students:

- Great job! Your analysis of the literature is insightful and thought-provoking.
- Your understanding of the literary devices used in the text is impressive.
- You have done a great job of identifying and analyzing the themes of the literature.
- Your responses to the literature are well-supported with evidence from the text.
- Your writing is clear and well-organized, making your analysis easy to follow.
- I appreciate the creative and unique perspective you bring to your analysis of the literature.
- Your use of figurative language in your writing helps to add depth and nuance to your analysis.
- Your analysis of the characters is perceptive and shows a deep understanding of their motivations and actions.
- You have a talent for drawing connections between different parts of the literature and synthesizing your ideas.
- Your writing is engaging and makes the reader want to keep reading.
- You have done a great job of considering the historical and cultural context of the literature in your analysis.
- I can see that you have put in a lot of effort to fully understand the text and its nuances.
- Your analysis of the literary elements helps to deepen the reader's understanding of the text.
- You have done a great job of using specific examples from the text to support your analysis.
- Keep up the great work! Your analysis of the literature is insightful and shows a deep engagement with the text.

CHAPTER SIXTY-EIGHT

Grammar and vocabulary usage feedback for students

Here are some grammar and vocabulary feedback comments that teachers could use to provide feedback to students:

- Excellent use of vocabulary! Your writing is rich and varied.
- Your sentence structure is strong and your grammar is accurate.
- You have done a great job of using context clues to determine the meanings of unfamiliar words.
- Your use of figurative language adds depth and nuance to your writing.
- I appreciate the care you have taken in proofreading your work for grammar and spelling errors.
- Your writing is clear and concise, making it easy to understand.
- You have a strong command of the English language and it shows in your writing.
- You have demonstrated a mastery of the grammar and vocabulary presented in class.
- Your writing shows a deep understanding of the nuances of the English language.
- Keep up the great work! Your writing is engaging and well-crafted.
- Your use of idioms and other expressions shows a high level of fluency in English.
- I can see that you have worked hard to expand your vocabulary and use it effectively in your writing.
- Your use of synonyms and antonyms helps to add variety to your writing.
- You have done a great job of using grammar and vocabulary to convey your ideas clearly and effectively.
- Your writing demonstrates a commitment to improving your grammar and vocabulary skills. Well done!

CHAPTER SIXTY-NINE

Feedback for Geometry Skills

Here are some geometry feedback comments that teachers could use to provide feedback to students:

- Excellent job! Your understanding of geometry concepts is strong.
- Your use of geometric formulas and calculations is accurate and precise.
- You have done a great job of identifying and applying geometric principles to solve problems.
- Your drawings and diagrams are clear and well-labeled, making it easy to understand your thought process.
- Your work shows strong attention to detail and a commitment to accuracy.
- Your understanding of spatial relationships is impressive.
- Your use of geometry to solve real-world problems shows a practical application of the concepts you have learned.
- You have a talent for visualizing and manipulating geometric shapes.
- Your use of different types of geometric transformations is impressive.
- Keep up the great work! Your ability to apply geometric concepts is impressive.
- Your use of logical reasoning in your geometric work is strong and clear.
- I appreciate the care you have taken in showing your work and explaining your reasoning.
- Your use of geometric principles to create and analyze designs is creative and impressive.
- Your understanding of the relationships between different geometric shapes is strong.
- Your work shows a deep engagement with the concepts of geometry and a commitment to mastering them. Well done!

CHAPTER SEVENTY

Feedback for Algebra

Here are some algebra feedback comments that teachers could use to provide feedback to students:

- Great job! Your understanding of algebraic concepts is strong.
- Your use of algebraic equations and formulas is accurate and precise.
- You have done a great job of identifying and solving algebraic problems.
- Your work shows strong attention to detail and a commitment to accuracy.
- Your use of algebra to solve real-world problems shows a practical application of the concepts you have learned.
- Your understanding of functions and their properties is impressive.
- Your use of logical reasoning in your algebraic work is strong and clear.
- You have a talent for identifying patterns and relationships in algebraic expressions.
- Your use of different algebraic operations is impressive.
- Keep up the great work! Your ability to apply algebraic concepts is impressive.
- Your use of algebraic expressions to create and analyze models is creative and impressive.
- I appreciate the care you have taken in showing your work and explaining your reasoning.
- Your use of algebraic principles to make predictions and draw conclusions is strong.
- Your understanding of the relationships between different algebraic expressions is strong.
- Your work shows a deep engagement with the concepts of algebra and a commitment to mastering them. Well done!

CHAPTER SEVENTY-ONE

Feedback for Science Project

Here are some science project feedback comments that teachers could use to provide feedback to students:

- Great job on your science project! You've shown a strong understanding of the scientific method.
- Your project is well-organized and clearly presented. It's easy to see how you went about conducting your experiment.
- Your data and results are presented clearly and accurately. Your tables and graphs are well-labeled and easy to read.
- You've done a great job of explaining your hypothesis and the reasoning behind it.
- Your project shows a good understanding of the scientific concepts involved.
- Your experimental design was thorough and well-planned.
- Your use of controls and variables was effective in helping to make your experiment reliable.
- Your conclusion is well-supported by your data and your analysis.
- You've shown creativity in choosing your project topic and designing your experiment.
- Keep up the good work! Your project is impressive and well-executed.
- Your project shows a clear understanding of cause-and-effect relationships.
- Your use of technology to collect and analyze data is impressive.
- You've done a great job of communicating your project and your findings to others.
- Your project shows a deep interest in and enthusiasm for science.
- Your work shows a strong commitment to the scientific process and to learning more about the world around us. Well done!

CHAPTER SEVENTY-TWO

Feedback for Art Work

Start with positive feedback. It's important to acknowledge the student's effort and creativity, and to highlight what you like about the work before diving into areas for improvement.

Be specific in your feedback. Instead of saying something general like "this is good," try to point out specific elements of the work that you appreciate, such as the use of color, the composition, or the level of detail.

Offer suggestions for improvement. If you see areas where the student could improve, try to offer constructive feedback that can help them grow as an artist. Be specific about what they could do differently and why it would improve the work.

Encourage the student to continue exploring and experimenting. Art is all about exploration and expression, so encourage the student to continue trying new things and pushing themselves creatively. Let them know that it's okay to make mistakes and that growth comes from taking risks and trying new things.

CHAPTER SEVENTY-THREE

Feedback for various MI skills (Multiple Intelligences)

Here are some specific feedback comments that you might find helpful when giving feedback on various multiple intelligences in students:

Verbal/Linguistic: If a student demonstrates strength in this area, they may be skilled at communicating their ideas through language. Feedback could include positive comments about their ability to express themselves well and use rich vocabulary, as well as suggestions for ways they could continue to develop their skills, such as exploring different writing styles or practicing public speaking.

Logical/Mathematical: If a student demonstrates strength in this area, they may be skilled at solving problems and thinking logically. Feedback could include positive comments about their ability to analyze and synthesize information, as well as suggestions for ways they could continue to develop their skills, such as exploring different problem-solving strategies or applying mathematical concepts to real-world situations.

Visual/Spatial: If a student demonstrates strength in this area, they may be skilled at visualizing and creating mental images. Feedback could include positive comments about their ability to think creatively and see things from different perspectives, as well as suggestions for ways they could continue to develop their skills, such as exploring different art forms or experimenting with design concepts.

Musical/Rhythmic: If a student demonstrates strength in this area, they may be skilled at creating and interpreting music and rhythms. Feedback could include positive comments about their ability to recognize patterns and rhythms, as well as suggestions for ways they could continue to develop their skills, such as exploring different musical genres or practicing improvisation.

Bodily/Kinaesthetic: If a student demonstrates strength in this area, they may be skilled at using their body and physical movement to express themselves. Feedback could include positive comments about their coordination and physicality, as well as suggestions for ways they could continue to develop their skills, such as exploring different dance styles or practicing yoga.

Interpersonal: If a student demonstrates strength in this area, they may be skilled at understanding and working well with others. Feedback could include positive comments about their ability to communicate effectively and build relationships, as well as suggestions for ways they could continue to develop their skills, such as practicing active listening or seeking out leadership opportunities.

Intrapersonal: If a student demonstrates strength in this area, they may be skilled at understanding their own thoughts, feelings, and motivations. Feedback could include positive comments about their ability to reflect on their own experiences and insights, as well as suggestions for ways they could continue to develop their skills, such as practicing self-care or exploring different mindfulness practices.

CHAPTER SEVENTY-FOUR

Feedback Comments on Rhyme Recitation

Here are some specific feedback comments that you might find helpful when giving feedback on reciting rhymes by students:

Focus on clarity and enunciation. Rhymes are often characterized by their rhythmic and rhyming patterns, so it's important for the student to speak clearly and enunciate each word in order to convey the full impact of the poem.

Comment on pacing and rhythm. Rhymes often have a distinct rhythm or tempo, and it's important for the student to find the right pace for the poem they are reciting. Feedback could include positive comments about the student's ability to maintain a consistent rhythm throughout the poem, as well as suggestions for areas where they could improve their pacing.

Note the emotional tone of the poem. Rhymes can be whimsical, serious, or emotional, and it's important for the student to capture the emotional tone of the poem in their recitation. Feedback could include positive comments about the student's ability to convey the emotions of the poem, as well as suggestions for areas where they could improve their delivery to enhance the emotional impact.

Highlight specific elements of the poem that stand out. Rhymes often have memorable lines or phrases that stick with the listener, and it's important for the student to highlight these elements in their recitation. Feedback could include positive comments about the student's ability to emphasize key phrases or words in the poem, as well as suggestions for ways they could continue to enhance their delivery of these elements.

Encourage the student to add their own flair. Reciting rhymes can be an opportunity for the student to showcase their personality and creativity. Encourage the student to experiment with different styles or interpretations of the poem, and to make the recitation their own.

CHAPTER SEVENTY-FIVE

Feedback for Storytelling

Here are some specific feedback comments that you might find helpful when giving feedback on storytelling for students:

Engaging opening. A good story starts with a captivating opening that draws the audience in. Feedback could include positive comments about the student's ability to engage the audience from the start, as well as suggestions for ways they could continue to develop their opening to create a stronger impact.

Clear plot and structure. A well-told story should have a clear plot and structure that is easy for the audience to follow. Feedback could include positive comments about the student's ability to organize their story effectively, as well as suggestions for ways they could continue to develop their storytelling skills to create a more compelling and coherent story.

Use of descriptive language. A good story should be vivid and engaging, with descriptive language that brings the story to life for the audience. Feedback could include positive comments about the student's ability to use descriptive language effectively, as well as suggestions for ways they could continue to develop their vocabulary and descriptive skills to create a richer, more immersive story.

Use of voice and expression. A well-told story should be delivered with confidence, using the voice and expression to convey the emotions and mood of the story. Feedback could include positive comments about the student's ability to use voice and expression effectively, as well as suggestions for ways they could continue to develop their delivery to create a more powerful and engaging performance.

Incorporating feedback. Encourage students to take feedback and incorporate it into their storytelling. Feedback could include positive comments about the student's ability to take constructive criticism and improve their storytelling based on feedback, as well as suggestions for areas where they could continue to improve.

CHAPTER SEVENTY-SIX

Feedback on Poster Making

Here are some specific feedback comments that you might find helpful when giving feedback on poster making:

Clear message. A good poster should communicate a clear message that is easy for the viewer to understand. Feedback could include positive comments about the student's ability to convey their message effectively, as well as suggestions for ways they could continue to refine their message to make it even clearer.

Use of color and design. A visually appealing poster can draw the viewer's attention and make the message more memorable. Feedback could include positive comments about the student's use of color and design, as well as suggestions for ways they could continue to experiment with different colors, fonts, and design elements to create a more visually striking poster.

Attention to detail. A well-made poster should demonstrate attention to detail, with a clean layout and high-quality graphics. Feedback could include positive comments about the student's attention to detail, as well as suggestions for ways they could continue to refine their design to create a more polished and professional-looking poster.

Creativity and originality. Encourage students to be creative and think outside the box when making their posters. Feedback could include positive comments about the student's creativity and originality, as well as suggestions for ways they could continue to experiment with different design ideas and incorporate their own unique style into their work.

Effective use of space. A good poster should use space effectively, with a clear hierarchy of information and a balance between text and graphics. Feedback could include positive comments about the student's use of space, as well as suggestions for ways they could continue to refine their layout to create a more effective poster.

CHAPTER SEVENTY-SEVEN

Feedback on Slogan Writing

Here are some specific feedback comments that you might find helpful when giving feedback on slogan writing:

Memorable and catchy. A good slogan should be memorable and catchy, with a message that sticks in the viewer's mind. Feedback could include positive comments about the student's ability to come up with a catchy slogan, as well as suggestions for ways they could continue to refine their message to make it even more memorable.

Clear message. A well-crafted slogan should convey a clear message that is easy for the viewer to understand. Feedback could include positive comments about the student's ability to communicate their message effectively, as well as suggestions for ways they could continue to refine their message to make it even clearer.

Use of language. Encourage students to experiment with different types of language, such as rhyme, alliteration, or puns, to create a more memorable and effective slogan. Feedback could include positive comments about the student's use of language, as well as suggestions for ways they could continue to experiment with different types of language to create more memorable and effective slogans.

Creativity and originality. A good slogan should be creative and original, standing out from other slogans in the same space. Feedback could include positive comments about the student's creativity and originality, as well as suggestions for ways they could continue to push the boundaries and come up with even more innovative slogans.

Adaptable to different contexts. A good slogan should be adaptable to different contexts, such as different audiences or different products. Feedback could include positive comments about the student's ability to create a versatile slogan, as well as suggestions for ways they could continue to refine their slogan to make it applicable in a variety of settings.

CHAPTER SEVENTY-EIGHT

Feedback on Roleplay

Here are some specific feedback comments that you might find helpful when giving feedback on role play:

Effective use of character. A good role play should involve a well-developed character that is consistent and believable throughout the performance. Feedback could include positive comments about the student's ability to create a compelling character, as well as suggestions for ways they could continue to develop their character to make it even more realistic and engaging.

Clear objective. A well-crafted role play should have a clear objective or goal that is communicated effectively to the audience. Feedback could include positive comments about the student's ability to communicate the objective effectively, as well as suggestions for ways they could continue to refine their objective to make it even clearer.

Use of dialogue. Dialogue is a key component of successful role-play, and good actors should be able to deliver their lines convincingly and in a natural manner. Feedback could include positive comments about the student's ability to deliver their lines effectively, as well as suggestions for ways they could continue to refine their dialogue to make it more authentic and engaging.

Use of body language. Encourage students to use body language to convey emotions and add depth to their performance. Feedback could include positive comments about the student's use of body language, as well as suggestions for ways they could continue to develop their physicality to create a more convincing and engaging performance.

Ability to improvise. A good role player should be able to think on their feet and improvise when necessary. Feedback could include positive comments about the student's ability to improvise effectively, as well as suggestions for ways they could continue to develop their improvisational skills to create a more dynamic and engaging performance.

CHAPTER SEVENTY-NINE

Feedback on Clay Moulding

Here are some specific feedback comments that you might find helpful when giving feedback on clay molding:

Attention to detail. A well-crafted clay mold should demonstrate attention to detail, with clean lines and a clear representation of the intended object or scene. Feedback could include positive comments about the student's attention to detail, as well as suggestions for ways they could continue to refine their mold to create a more polished and professional-looking final product.

Use of texture. Texture is an important component of clay molding, and good sculptors should be able to use texture effectively to create a more realistic and engaging final product. Feedback could include positive comments about the student's use of texture, as well as suggestions for ways they could continue to experiment with different types of texture to create more dynamic and engaging molds.

Proportion and scale. A good clay mold should accurately represent the proportion and scale of the intended object or scene. Feedback could include positive comments about the student's ability to represent proportion and scale accurately, as well as suggestions for ways they could continue to refine their molds to make them even more realistic.

Creativity and originality. Encourage students to be creative and think outside the box when making their molds. Feedback could include positive comments about the student's creativity and originality, as well as suggestions for ways they could continue to experiment with different design ideas and incorporate their own unique style into their work.

Use of tools. Sculpting tools are an important part of clay molding, and good sculptors should be able to use their tools effectively to create the desired effect. Feedback could include positive comments about the student's use of tools, as well as suggestions for ways they could continue to develop their tool skills to create more intricate and detailed molds

CHAPTER EIGHTY

Feedback for Effective Library Usage

Here are some specific feedback comments that you might find helpful when giving feedback on effective library usage by students:

Use of resources. A good library user should be able to identify and effectively use a variety of resources to meet their research needs. Feedback could include positive comments about the student's ability to identify and use appropriate resources, as well as suggestions for ways they could continue to explore new resources and expand their research skills.

Organization and time management. Effective library usage requires good organizational and time management skills. Feedback could include positive comments about the student's ability to manage their time effectively while conducting research, as well as suggestions for ways they could continue to develop these skills to improve their efficiency and productivity.

Research skills. A good library user should be able to conduct effective research, including identifying research questions, developing search strategies, and evaluating sources. Feedback could include positive comments about the student's research skills, as well as suggestions for ways they could continue to develop these skills to become even more effective researchers.

Respect for resources. Encourage students to treat library resources with respect, including returning materials on time, handling materials carefully, and following library policies and procedures. Feedback could include positive comments about the student's respect for library resources, as well as suggestions for ways they could continue to be responsible library users and ambassadors for the library.

Collaboration and communication. Effective library usage often requires collaboration and communication, whether working with a librarian or with fellow students on a research project. Feedback could include positive comments about the student's ability to work collaboratively and communicate effectively with others while using the library, as well as suggestions for ways they could continue to develop these skills to become even more effective researchers and team members.

CHAPTER EIGHTY-ONE

Feedback for Creativity and Innovation

Here are some sample remarks for creativity and innovation for students:

Bold Thinking: [Student Name] has demonstrated a fearless approach to problem-solving and an ability to think outside the box. Their innovative ideas have challenged conventional thinking and resulted in unique and creative solutions.

Resourcefulness: [Student Name] has shown great resourcefulness in their approach to projects and assignments. They have demonstrated an ability to work with limited resources and find creative solutions to overcome obstacles and challenges.

Originality: [Student Name] has consistently shown originality in their work. Their unique perspectives and unconventional ideas have resulted in impressive and innovative projects.

Experimentation: [Student Name] has demonstrated a willingness to take risks and experiment with new ideas and concepts. Their curiosity and eagerness to learn have resulted in original and creative projects.

Collaborative Creativity: [Student Name] has shown great creativity in their collaborative efforts. They have worked effectively with others to generate innovative solutions and ideas, and have been a positive influence on their team's creativity.

Passion: [Student Name] has shown a genuine passion for creative endeavors. Their enthusiasm and dedication have inspired others and contributed to the creative atmosphere of our school community.

Creative Presentation: [Student Name] has consistently demonstrated a talent for presenting their ideas in a creative and engaging way. Their innovative approach to presentation has resulted in memorable and impactful projects.

CHAPTER EIGHTY-TWO

Feedback for Problem-Solving Skills

Here are some sample feedback comments for problem-solving skills:

Creative Solutions: [Student Name] consistently demonstrates an ability to generate creative solutions to complex problems. Their unique perspectives and willingness to think outside the box have resulted in innovative and effective problem-solving.

Logical Thinking: [Student Name] has shown exceptional logical thinking skills when approaching problems. They are able to break down complex issues into manageable parts and work systematically to find solutions.

Perseverance: [Student Name] has shown great perseverance when faced with difficult problems. They are determined to find solutions and do not give up easily. Their tenacity has resulted in successful outcomes.

Collaboration: [Student Name] works effectively with others to solve problems. They are able to listen to different perspectives, communicate clearly, and contribute effectively to group problem-solving efforts.

Critical Thinking: [Student Name] has demonstrated strong critical thinking skills in their approach to problem-solving. They are able to evaluate information, identify potential roadblocks, and make informed decisions based on evidence.

Risk-Taking: [Student Name] has shown a willingness to take risks when approaching problems. They are not afraid to try new approaches and take calculated risks in order to find solutions.

Resourcefulness: [Student Name] has shown great resourcefulness when solving problems. They are able to find creative solutions with limited resources and work within constraints to find effective solutions.

End Note

In conclusion, I hope that this book on feedback to feedforward has provided valuable insights and practical strategies for educators of all grades. My aim in writing this book was to help educators understand the importance of providing effective feedback to their students and to provide them with the tools and resources they need to do so.

I firmly believe that by adopting feedback to feedforward approach, educators can help students take ownership of their learning, identify areas for improvement, and make positive changes that will support their academic growth and development.

I would like to thank all of our readers for their interest in this book and for their commitment to supporting student learning. I hope that the strategies and insights provided in these pages will help you to become more effective feedback providers and to make a positive impact on the lives of your students.

Finally, I would like to extend my best wishes to all educators and students as they continue on their academic journey. May you continue to learn, grow, and achieve your goals, with the support and guidance of effective feedback to feedforward.

Mentoring The Mentors

Mentoring The Mentors is a highly regarded YouTube channel for educators hosted by Dr. Meenakshi Narula. Dr. Narula is an experienced educator and author with a passion for helping other educators develop their teaching skills and strategies.

Through her YouTube channel, Dr. Narula shares her expertise on a range of topics related to education, including effective feedback strategies, student engagement, and teacher development. Her videos are highly informative, engaging, and practical, making them an invaluable resource for educators at all levels.

One of the key strengths of Mentoring The Mentors is Dr. Narula's ability to break down complex concepts into simple, easy-to-understand language. This makes her videos accessible to educators with a range of experience levels, from those who are just starting out to those who are more experienced.

In addition to her educational videos, Dr. Narula also offers personalized coaching and mentoring services for educators who are looking to take their teaching to the next level. Her coaching sessions are tailored to meet the specific needs and goals of each individual educator and provide them with the support and guidance they need to achieve their full potential.

Overall, Mentoring the Mentors is an outstanding resource for educators who are committed to their own professional development and to the success of their students. Dr. Narula's expertise, experience, and passion for teaching make her an exceptional mentor and coach, and her YouTube channel is an excellent platform for sharing her knowledge and insights with educators around the world.

Mentoring The Mentor

Our Motto- "to Accelerate Your Learning Curve"

The motto "Accelerate Your Learning Curve" is an expression that emphasizes the importance of learning and continuous improvement in achieving personal and professional goals.

The term "learning curve" originally referred to the rate at which a person becomes proficient at a new skill or task over time. The steeper the learning curve, the faster the rate of improvement. The motto "Accelerate Your Learning Curve" implies that by intentionally seeking out new knowledge, skills, and experiences, and by applying oneself diligently to the process of learning, one can achieve more rapid progress and success.

The concept of accelerating one's learning curve can be applied to many areas of life, from personal hobbies to professional development. It encourages individuals to seek out challenges, take risks, and to be open to new perspectives and ideas.

By embracing the motto "Accelerate Your Learning Curve," individuals can cultivate a growth mindset, which is the belief that one's abilities can be developed through dedication and hard work. This mindset fosters a willingness to embrace challenges, persevere through difficulties, and learn from failures.

Ultimately, the motto "Accelerate Your Learning Curve" is a call to action to take charge of one's own learning and development, and to pursue personal and professional growth with intention and purpose.

9 798889 865278

Printed by Libri Plureos GmbH in Hamburg,
Germany